I0762306

Goose River Anthology, 2009

Edited by

Deborah J. Benner

Goose River Press
Waldoboro, Maine

Library of Congress Card Number: 2009907536

ISBN: 978-1-59713-085-1

First Printing, 2009

Cover photo by Kasey Benner

Published by
Goose River Press
3400 Friendship Road
Waldoboro ME 04572
gooseriverpress@roadrunner.com
www.gooseriverpress.com

Table of Contents

Table of Contents

Table of Contents

Table of Contents

In Loving Memory of

My Dad

Donald E. Simmons, Sr.

Dec. 18, 1936 - Feb. 10, 2009

Goose River Anthology, 2009

Sally Belenardo
Branford, CT

When Redwings Return

One day,
between the end of day
and nightfall,
light rises from the woods
and lingers
between peach and rose

and from low woodland
between snow and water
rises the burbling sound
of blackbirds singing
between the end of winter
and the blush of spring,
between hunger of the hart*
and flow of maple blood;

from wetland
between ice and water
rises the burbling song of redwings
between sunset and nightfall
when light lingers
between peach and gold

and while I listen
to the risen song,
between the crimson light
and quiet cold of fallen night,
my longing for the end of winter ends.

*hart: deer/stag

Emily Ellis
Lewiston, ME

Leaving the Schoolyard

Discarded paper blowing in an empty lot
one at my feet, equations
on an unnamed sheet
was credit given
or denied?
My gaze fixed downward
feel the hapless bulge inside my bag
farewell gifts with handshakes
gestures innocent, innocuous
"it wasn't us who let you go."

Whirr of motors humming
as she leans far in to kiss him
nothing else exists nor should
as now her image, bolder
in my memory
than in my room, then so alone
so needy.

Is it my turn now, to seek
warm arms in waiting car
to hold against a gnarling rage
embrace till fog enfolds
all glass, all that casts shadow
on advancing age

Emily Ellis
Lewiston, ME

Yet, as I stare,
outline in air space held
within
hear frantic scurrying of feet
outside my door
voices, strained, diluted
muted information
not for sharing unless
asked
world of loops and circles
dangling in a geometric web of
anonymity
what worth a name
without an anchor.

Browning grass on a graying day
somewhere a key, a pen, a stick of gum
slightest traces of one's passing

tomorrow opens
on the boot heels of today
kicking knots of sodden dirt,
then starting up
driving away.

Gene Rackovitch
Greenport, NY

A Marine

Calibers: rounds per second: as far as the eye can see,
tracers, fundamentals, functionary, basics, procedure, fire
power, squad coordinates, blossoms to Armies, evaluations,
flanking movements, attack, point, rear guard. I am an
instrument, an equation, an expendable,
through death, peeked altruism, authoritarianism,
abandoned self and soul.
Far away, gray winter and full blossom summer, whisking
by, spring, rolling farm land. America,
replaced for skull and cross bones, in far off lands.
Obligations to mankind, to humanity, flag and country;
none of these, pleasures of grit to cleansing, pores alive,
adrenal feeding
The soul of another I have taken, 30 caliber sealing death.
A brave man, no
What quits necessity?
What fathoms right?
Here I be, souls of those I exterminated entering my body.
Oh Lord what is right, what is just?
God, thy help I have asked,
but still uncertainty propels.
Oh God, depart the soul of another from my body.
So it is for self determination.
The inequity of affecting death.
The quality of being my brother's keeper.
What you try to understand these writings?
Leave be!
The malady of this Marine stands before you.
The malady of a single man is written here.
Semper Fidelis

Rosemarie Nervelle
Camden, ME

Saying Goodbye

There was an obvious sneer of disgust on the guard's slack lips as he slammed shut the cell door behind the shabbily dressed old woman. With outstretched arms and tear-stained cheeks, she buried her face in her son's shoulder and convulsed with sobs.

"Oh, Mamma, please don't cry. I asked you not to come here. I don't want you seein' me like this; caged like some animal. Oh, but Mamma, I'm so glad to see you. 'Course I knew you'd come. Yes, you and I both know I was railroaded. Hey, come on now, sit down on my bunk. Let me take your coat. Yes, that's fine. Feel better now?

Mamma, you're the only one who believes I didn't kill Jenny. Like I told them folks on the jury, it all happened so fast. We was just settin' on the porch at sundown, talkin' an' laughin' like we always did when she was feelin' good. She was stitchin' somethin'. Her sewin' basket was right there beside her chair. I said somethin', somethin' innocent and soothin' like I always did when I talked to Jenny. I can't even remember what I said. But somethin' came over her real sudden. Her face changed between the time I said what I said and the last time I glanced over at her, sittin' stitchin' in her chair, so tranquil and peaceful. She didn't even look like herself. I asked her what ailed her, worried that she might be havin' some kind of spell. She grabbed them scissors from the basket and come at me with the most awful look in her eyes. I tried to talk calm to her, to tell her that I understood how she was feelin'. It was no good, Mamma. She kept comin' at me with them scissors, screamin' and swearin'. She wasn't herself. She just...wasn't herself. You know I wouldn't never hurt a hair on Jenny's head.... Well, maybe I did shake her up once or twice; only 'cause she'd get hysterical when the devil got into her.

Rosemarie Nervelle
Camden, ME

"You know how much I loved her, don't you? She was the only woman I ever truly and honestly loved next to you, and I just knew right off that I couldn't live without her.

She was so sweet and thoughtful and lovin'. I still can't believe how fast it all just seemed to get out of control. Seems like the devil just got into her without warnin', without provocation. The reverend said she was 'possessed' with some kind of demon. I believe him 'cause that's what it seemed like.

"That prosecutor, he said I killed her 'cause I was tired of takin' care of her. You know that ain't true, don't you, Mamma? When she took sick, didn't I keep her home with me instead of puttin' her away in that sanitarium where her daddy died? Now, I wish to God I had...'cause I thought about it when she got worse, too late.

"The folks on that jury; why couldn't they believe Jenny fell on them scissors? No witness was there when she come at me. It was a real freakish accident, I know. It was like somethin' put itself between Jenny and me, somethin' solid but invisible and she fell over it. Was it God tripped her up, Mamma? Or was it the devil? Would God save me from them scissors, then take poor Jenny's life just to have me die in the electric chair? Or was it the devil that kept tormentin' her, got tired of his old toy, then started in on me? Wish I knew.

"Oh, Mamma, your prayers can't save me now. When I was twenty-one, you told me, 'Son, you're a man now. You can be whatever you want.' But, that ain't so, Mamma. I could only be what God and the world let me be. I ain't had the wherewithal to be nothin' else. I got married, too young, like you said, and just took care of Jenny. I ain't complainin', mind you. We had a real good time before she took sick. I think about her all the time. I wake up in this cell in the early mornin' and know the only thing different about it is me bein' one more day closer to my Jenny.

"I just been countin' down the days for three years here on death row, but today is my last day. Tonight I get anything

Rosemarie Nervelle
Camden, ME

I want for supper. Bet you can't guess what I asked for.

"No ma'am, not steak. Lobster! I asked for lobster. I ain't never had me a lobster in my whole life. I ain't never flew in a' airplane neither. Never had no kids. Never seen New York City, or the ocean, a' elephant. Never, never...and I never will.

"Oh, I think about you, too, Mamma. How hard you worked. Standin' at the bus stop in this same old black coat, shiverin' in the cold, ankles all swollen. Keepin' us all together, always waitin' up and stickin' up for us. When you come right down to it, your life ain't been no bed of roses, has it? Tomorrow mornin' my troubles'll be over, but you'll still be carryin' yours: 'The mother of the man executed for killin' his crazy wife.' Don't matter to nobody it was the will of God wantin' Jenny and me to be together forever.

"Now, don't you cry, hear? If you think about it, it's gonna be all right. I'm gonna be with my Jenny. Oh, look. Here's the man bringin' my supper. They're gonna make you leave now. Funny thing, though. I think I done lost my appetite.

"I love you, too. Bye, Mamma. Goodbye."

F. Anthony D'Alessandro
Orlando, FL

Last Game

The jump shot swishes, barely brushing the rim.
Scoreboard registers two more.
Is that all there is? He wonders.
The senior, swarmed by teammates as he lopes toward the
soppy bench,
remains speechless in the mouth of mayhem.
A dozen pimpled backs stand; two dozen hands clap with
the voice of one.
The fuzzy faced freshman runs onto the parquet floor for
his debut.

After a round of high fives, the scarecrow haired player
squints at the game clock.
Eyes fixed; he loiters, biting down on dry lips.
He hangs his drooling jacket over freckled shoulders, and
sits droopy headed.
A few moments later, he searches the peeling crowd,
and stands dazzled by undulating fingers of light,
so different from his cratered, tree crowded backyard court.
Searching beyond shapes and shadows, he focuses on his
most enduring fan.
The boy winks.

Suddenly, he's back to kerosene winters, dank gymnasia,
decorated with dangling ropes,
his first behind the back dribble, his opponent and best pal
falling
while writhing in laughter and,
a toothy faced, well-postured black beard winking, a
twinkle in his look.

(continued)

F. Anthony D'Alessandro
Orlando, FL

They'd not planned for this hoop ball curtain to fall with
such finality.
There was no warning and no encore.
The game would never end, so thought the boy and dad.

Sporting a soft, fuzzy chin,
the boy swaggers off the mirrored basketball court.
With moodiness trickling from his soul, the boy speaks thru
a raspy voice.
"Pop," he says with raised brow, "for most of my life, from
my eighth birthday to my twenty-first year, I've suited for
this game. Is that all there is?"
His biggest fan resorts to tip toes, and plants a kiss on his
boy's dripping cheek.
Then, the player wipes off the mix of sweat and tears,
arm draped around a slumping, steely bearded father.

***

Nancy Galland
Stockton Springs, ME

Chairs

Chairs sit and wait;
arms held out to hold,
a place to rest the back,
to raise the buttocks
safely off the ground,
a place to rest the wrist,
a chance to bend the knee,
to rest one leg upon another.
Chairs sit and wait to receive,
sometimes to cradle-rock again.

Catherine Wang Hsu
Malden, MA

Sarcasm

Sarcasm is the thing,
soft with lace
that veils
a sharp knife.

That cuts the
heart
and cries the
laugh.

That slashes the
sore
and shows no
blood.

That pinpoints the
point
and never
points
at all!

Fred Farris
Leawood, KS

Cello Bells

A skinny boy about fourteen bounced out of a white Chevy van as it rolled to a stop in front of the red brick duplex. As the landlord hammered a "For Rent" sign in the front yard, the boy approached. He had that wave-surfer look; sandy hair swooped across his forehead, and a black string necklace around his tanned neck.

"Sir, may my father and mother look at the apartment?" he asked. "We're just moving into town." The landlord arched one bushy white eyebrow.

A slim woman and a jut-jawed man stepped out of the van.

"This is my mom and dad, Ingrid and Thor Johanssen," the boy said. "They are both deaf. My name is Erik." He extended his right hand.

Turning toward his parents Erik flashed flying fingers signaling the landlord gave permission to look inside. Glancing at the landlord, the boy said, "I'm sure you'd like to know they both have jobs, they work at the State School for the Deaf here in town."

"That's good," the old landlord said.

Erik bounded up the stairs into the second bedroom like a Viking explorer. *My room,* he thought as he planned where his computer and ball-bearing skateboard would go.

On the first of every month, Erik phoned the landlord; "Your rent is ready sir." Erik also called when the air conditioner, furnace or plumbing needed repair. His easy smile soon elected him crown prince of the other kids on the block in their skateboard racing down to the 7-Eleven store.

Erik asked the landlord's permission for his dad to build a wooden roller skateboard ramp in the back yard. He practiced his skating jumps on the big curved hardwood bowl. His shaggy ragtop, rocket-fueled by kinetic energy, rolled up

Fred Farris
Leawood, KS

above the top of the rim nearly completing a full twist in the air before landing back on his feet in a plummeting descent.

"Holy crap Erik," yelled his buddy, Joe, "You're gonna wipe out if you try that again."

"I can do it!" Erik yelled, "I'm a Viking voyager."

In his sophomore year at high school, Erik wanted to play in the school orchestra, but worried that his dad wouldn't give permission. At breakfast Erik used his most articulate signing semantics to plead his case for joining the big string orchestra.

"No," his dad signed back, "all the extra practice required will take time from your neighborhood grass cutting jobs."

The next day Erik asked his music teacher, Mrs. Martin, "How can I possibly describe what an orchestra sounds like to my dad?"

> E-mail Sept 10
> From: Jane Martin, North High School
> To Thor and Ingrid Johanssen
>
> Your son is an eager student and his interest in music is very important to him. Music training will add discipline and enjoyment to his life long after his school years. I hope you will allow him to join our class. He wants to play the cello. You may be able to feel the vibration (the music) by putting your hand on the cello as he practices at home.

The next day his dad, after a little push from his mom, said, "Okay, if that's what you both want, but you'll have to mow some extra lawns to help pay for the cello's cost."

By a year later, Erik had earned promotion to first chair in the four-cello section. He played with near rapture on his beautiful cherry-wood cello. Gliding his bow back and forth across the strings with the cello cradled between his legs,

Fred Farris
Leawood, KS

launched waves of vibrating caresses on his knees and thighs. Deep rhythmic tones raced up through his body, heart and head. The sounds also drowned out an annoying buzzing ring in his ears, an irritating sound that was definitely not written on the musical score.

After performing in the year-end concert for parents, Erik stood with the orchestra and bowed to audience applause. He thought, *Those extra bell noises in my head didn't interfere as much as I expected.* At home he announced he had decided to try out for the Greater Kansas City Area Youth Symphony.

The boy yearned to be able to explain to his mom and dad what the magic of music sounds like. But he could no more do it than when he once tried describing the drone of cicadas in the back yard, or explain the thrill of a John Phillips Sousa march.

When the bell noises in his ears continued, Erik asked his buddy Joe, whose mom taught at the Deaf School, if he ever heard little strange noises in his head?

"Are you nuts?" Joe yelped, then seeing the embarrassed downturn of Erik's eyes, Joe understood. He added, "I'll ask my mom for you, but don't worry, I won't tell her why I'm asking."

A week later Joe reported back, "Tinnitus, my mom called it," he said, "its tinkling bell sounds or a windy whistle in the inner ear; it'll probably go away, don't worry about it."

As the following summer drifted into October, Erik paused in the middle of a neighbor's lawn. He turned off the mower engine to rake and bag. He reached down and picked up a pencil-thin stick fallen from a tree. Tapping it on the mower handle three times for attention, he glided his baton vigorously through eight bars at allegro tempo. Underfoot, golden leaves crackled a snare drum riff; over head a flock of Mallards honked their woodwind wails; a staccato of barking dogs augmented the melody and the Santa Fe train whistle three blocks east added its oboe solo.

Fred Farris
Leawood, KS

He paused, then flung his baton on the ground as he became acutely aware that the train whistle sounded less loud this year and he realized it wasn't the train's fault. Even so it was still nature's music set in beautiful cadence and framed in pure colors of the Master Director.

"You missed another entrance on that down beat, Erik," Mrs. Martin said at rehearsal. He winced.

As the landlord parked his black Buick at the curb, Erik skipped down the front steps; his hair overflowed his head like golden froth on a glass of root beer. It floated to rest at the car door. He handed the landlord his monthly envelope containing the rent in crisp one-hundred dollar bills. As he waited for a receipt he asked.

"What do you do with all this money sir?"

"Most of it goes to the bank to repay the mortgage loan they gave me."

"Maybe I'll be a landlord someday."

"Maybe you will become a real estate tycoon; you even look like Donald Trump."

The landlord cracked a thin grin.

A few weeks later, Erik lost his first chair position. Inwardly crushed, he scowled at Mrs. Martin. After another three rehearsals, he thought maybe he'd switch to playing the big bass so he could slap and beat the instrument hard enough to drive that devil out of his head.

Summer drifted into autumn like a lazy lyric. After dinner Erik rose from the table. "Gotta go, Mom," he signed a finger-twisting, "thanks for dinner." He pushed up the garage door and wheeled his lawn mower down Walnut Street to a waiting overgrown lawn. An amber sun slipped below the western horizon into twilight as he got home. Grabbing his skateboard, he zoomed off a full aerial twist, but the thrill was gone. A low-pitched whistling ring sounded in his right ear. Corrosive thoughts ran free-footed through his fertile mind, *If I go deaf I won't be able to help Mom and Dad.... Is it my fault?*

Fred Farris
Leawood, KS

He turned to practicing Mrs. Martin's newly assigned Beethoven sonata for the coming concert. It required double fingering, the hardest kind to learn. Mrs. Martin kept telling how Beethoven went deaf. Why couldn't she stick with Haydn and Handel like last year? He hated Beethoven, but he was confident he could do it if those bells would just stop for a little while.

That night in bed, a green pinpoint of light from his computer across the room flashed on/off, on/off. The little dot now grew into a giant eyeball like the CBS Eye. It lasered a burning beam into his brain. Now the blinking light transformed into pulsing, pounding, chiming bell-towers in both ears—like Hell's heart throbbing. He rose, sat at the computer and turned it on. It's fluorescent screen saturated the dark bedroom with an ominous glow. He typed a lone pleading word, WHY? All his senses, for a time confused, plunged in a sinking quicksand of gloom. His heart sank with them. He banged the computer with cuss words to express his confused anguish. The bells grew louder joined by a whooshing whistling whirlwind.

Clamping his hands over his ears, his brain reeled and rang like a merry-go-round calliope. *WHY is this strange torment in my head? Why me? Now I'll never make the symphony.*

The sweet smell of success began to smell more like ammonia; impossible to breathe. Banging bells finally faded as he fell into merciful sleep.

The day after his 16th birthday Erik received his driver's license and went driving with his dad. Later, after mowing, Erik returned to his own driveway. He pushed up the rolling overhead garage door and wheeled the mower in next to his dad's Chevy. As he reached up and pulled down the old garage door it screamed a tortured cry for help as it banged shut on the concrete floor.

Erik opened the van door on the driver's side, climbed in and sat in the driver's seat. The key glinted in the ignition.

Fred Farris
Leawood, KS

He started the engine...a double gong reverberated on both eardrums drowning out the sound of the motor. More clanging now like a fire engine bell rang in his right ear. Like a caged animal seeking escape, he pleaded, *Where are they coming from? From outside? From inside? From Hell? I've got to shut them out.* He rolled up the car windows...the bells seemed quieter now and less frequent. Sighing deeply...he leaned back into the comfortable seat...sighed again...and closed his eyes.

From the outside his dad rolled the garage door up.

"Oh my God." He ran to the car, jerked the door open, grabbed Erik's shirt and shook him. The boy slumped sideward into his dad's arms. His dad dragged him outside and shook Erik again. His eyelids fluttered open. Prone on the driveway, father and son hugged, both sobbing as Erik coughed and gulped fresh air.

"Why...WHY ?" his dad signed. Erik looked up into his eyes. *How could he explain?* Erik clenched both fists and pounded them on his own ears. He reached his hands up, grabbed both his dad's ears and pulled on them.

"PAIN," he signed. His dad winced.

"We will help you!" The reply came silently like a prayer

Next semester, the final strains of Tschaikovsky's Serenade for Strings triggered an avalanche of applause. All members of The Greater Kansas City Youth Symphony stood for their recognition. The first chair cellist's eyes misted over. Erik raised his cello bow once again. He stretched out his arm, pointing his bow directly toward three people in the audience. His white-haired ear doctor and his parents bolted out of their seats, arms raised like a football touchdown. A thousand applauding hands resounded new hope in Erik's ears.

Helen Vandepeer
Pembroke, Ontario

Chopin

Outside snow falls, silent diaphanous crystals.
I'll not venture out today.
Chopin plays—
a gift of love at Christmas time.

My man sleeps upon the couch.
The house is quiet and at peace.
This beautiful cottage—
where love and laughter abound
The portions equal.

Gracious it is, full or color, flowers in every room
Chopin continues with music sweet.
The snow continues—
The landscape whitens
The beloved blanket-covered one sleeps on.

Music tempo quickens.
Snow falls faster, thicker—
the two in amazing synchronicity.
I retreat from the window where I watch.
Soup bubbling in a pot.

Chopin's gift of melody to mankind plays on.
Such peace, such joy.
Such days are mine.

Ken Keith
San Diego, CA

Landlocked

"It was the raft and mighty glad was we
to get aboard of it again."
—Mark Twain

My little brother poles with a broken branch,
pushing hard to free our half-swamped
little bridgeplank raft
from the slimy mud of this shallow
landlocked Iowa pig farm pond,
not yet out of sight of house and barn,
under the sharp eye of an old hawk
perched high atop a telephone pole,
head gyrating slowly to watch us
circling in brown water like desperate fish
in a rusty rain barrel,
on our way to Silver Creek and the Nishna,
on down to the Missouri
and the great confluence at St. Louie,
keeping one eye out for Huck and Jim,
the other on the thunderheads roiling
in the southwestern Iowa sky
and threatening at any moment
to fill our rubber boots and Big Smith overalls
with enough sharp-edged summer sleet
to drown our sorry butts
before we get home to feed the hogs.

Philip Pendleton
Camden, ME and Melrose, MA

In Praise of Letter Writing

When was the last time you received a real letter via the U.S. mail? Yes, I know that most, if not all of you are thinking. "Doesn't this guy know that letter writing went out years ago?"

Okay, okay. But to me there's nothing like receiving a letter in the mail, and sitting down and reading it at my leisure. I'm very fortunate because once or twice a month I receive a handwritten letter from my former third grade teacher who is 100 years old! It's full of chatty items about the social events she's been to, being taken out to meals three times a week with different groups of friends, the status of her health, etc. These letters I cherish dearly, and I save every one.

It may be that my zest for letters is hereditary. In our old farm house in Camden, Maine I have found literally hundreds of letters and postcards. Many were from my grandmother (it was almost always the woman who did the writing) to her daughters. Granted most of them were centered on talking about the weather, what they were eating, etc., but occasionally a gem showed up. For example, my Aunt Evie wrote from Thomasville, Georgia where her husband was working, that she had just rented a piano. I had no idea that her love for music was that strong. Another example was a letter from my grandmother to her daughter describing what a fine time they were having with Gramp Barnes' sister and husband in Southbridge, Mass. Till I read that I had no idea that my grandparents had ever been out of the state of Maine.

World War II brought on a tremendous volume of letter writing. I received a few letters from people I barely knew, wishing me well. When I went overseas, V mail predominated. These were letters put on tape in small cylinders. They

Philip Pendleton
Camden, ME and Melrose, MA

were then printed out when they reached their destination. This process saved much space in transportation.

Letters from troops overseas were always censored to make sure that nothing affecting security was in them. Occasionally the officer censoring the mail would excise something with scissors. I was present at an amusing event one day when the officer read aloud (but without identifying the writer), “Boy, would I like to go tenting with Ingrid Bergman!” Very unsophisticated times then.

Now back to the present. Yes, email is fine, and I use it all the time. But how often is something printed out that will be saved and passed on to the next generation? I close with a challenge to you: Sit down and write a letter to a close relative or a good friend. Tell him or her something significant that has happened to you. Perhaps a major move and a change, or loss of a job, and how you felt about it. Or it might be the death of a person and why that person meant so much to you. It could be describing the best, or the worst thing that has ever happened to you. These are messages the recipient will save forever and will pass on to his or her children.

Go to it! Shut off the email and write a real letter!

Robert Witte
Waldoboro, ME

The Salt-Marsh

A firefall of sun, then
swift and soft a watercall
of ducks across the marsh and
swampland, rippling dusk and wind
along the water winding spaces
of its tall-reed sighings for the night.

One small silver undulation gleam,
light goes away from water,
from violet sky, and night drifts in
between the reeds, a tidal salt-mud smell.

The bittern booms—once,
so short his time, for dusk is gone;
black gouache night, and estuarine eels
slide silky, rippling,
in the black backwaters of the swamp.

Diana Woodcock
Doha, QATAR & Midlothian, VA

First Thing You Must Do

Upon arrival: seek them out.
Learn to identify them

in scrub, on limb.
Call them by name.

Distinguish between residents,
passage migrants, winter

visitors. Check out their
histories: range extenders;

escapees; fortunate ones
released from captivity.

They'll be your lifeline here.
Surrounded by desert—

waste ground, endless shades
of brown—suddenly, if

lucky, you'll spot a sulphur—
crested cockatoo or a streaked

weaver, and your heart will leap
the desert's ties.

If it fails to do so, you'll
know it's turned to stone,

and you've lost all hope of
the desert becoming home.

Russell Crabtree
Rockland, ME

Fog

So many people find a foggy day so depressing.
Not so do I.
The sky is not gray—but argent.
The lowering skies reach down to touch the land
with a life giving, misty caress
that I too feel upon my cheek.

Sky and silvery calm waters become
one in the near distance.
The water's surface is rippled in serene symmetry
by the unhurried passage of a loon.
The multitude of greens become deeper
and seemingly more lush.

Sounds are muted, silhouettes are softened.
Every meadow becomes infinite in depth
and mysterious.
A brilliant summer day becomes hushed
and tranquil.

Dawn Edwards
Melrose, MA

Where or When

She sits expectantly, lightly
As though waiting to be asked to dance
Queen of the Lindy, the Jive, the Bop
Soldiers stood in line for just one chance

She smiles vacantly at the photos
Dashing groom in dress uniform, "Who
Is the lovely bride all silk and lace,
I don't know that couple dear, do you?"

She hums to the tune *On Moonlight Bay*
Her three children visit when they can
Son Tony doesn't know what to say
When he comes she asks, "Who is that man?"

She seems happy floating through her mind
And spends her day folding clothes, singing,
Chatting chatter to faces like hers
And in between, memories ling'ring.

Marc J. Seifer
Kingston, RI

The Graphologue

Dressed smartly in a charcoal grey three-piece pin-striped suit, Jacob Bruno stared out the pigeon stained window of his office, a second story walk up, combination class room, graphology and rare manuscript bookstore, between 61st and 62nd on Lexington Avenue, and burst into tears. “Oh, Sollie!,” he wailed, as he turned to gaze at the one and only framed, wrinkled, photo of his wife and son that survived the war. His only son frozen for eternity at eight years of age, Solomon Isaiah Bruno, with his thin brown hair cascading out from under his grandfather’s tureen-shaped yarmulke, curled *peyes* spiraling down about his ears, trusting hazel eyes and innocent face, sitting on his mother’s lap, smiling up at Papa. Deep waves of grief poured through the old man’s being as he thought back to that black day when Sollie died in his arms. In the midst of a cold snap. In The Camp. Just twenty days before his release. February, 1939. “Why didn’t you take me?” he sobbed as his eyes turned back towards the window to watch a peregrine falcon snatch a pigeon from a flock as it banked sharply to avoid a highrise as it landed at its nest atop a nearby three-story townhouse. With his own weight down to 84 pounds, it was a miracle that he survived, that anyone made it out, if you could call it that. But Sollie was below 60 pounds, a skeleton that hardly breathed. Like Hollenschtein, who attempted suicide, and two other Buchenwald survivors who succeeded in leaving this hell called earth, Jacob Bruno remained at his core, another of the walking dead waiting for the reunion with his family.

“Jacob,” Shirley’s voice came over the intercom. “Your 2 o’clock is here...Jacob, are you there?”

“Give me a minute,” he paused, “to vash up, and zen show her in. And call up Hollenschtein. I’ll meet him for dinner at seven.”

Marc J. Seifer
Kingston, RI

Overweight Shirley, in her Rosemary Clooney autumn-colored muumuu, eased herself into the room, closing the door quietly behind. "You saw him last week." She raised both eyebrows in a pleading gesture. "He only makes you depressed."

"We're za only dead ones left, now. Maybe we'll just finish each other off, like we planned. A Heaven's Gate cocktail. It'll make God happy."

"That wasn't God's doing," she responded weakly.

"Nevertheless, people died, including young men and women and particularly children. A few, like my Sollie, starved to death. But most were gassed, or mowed down with machine guns, or better yet, experimented on, raped and zen fed to the dogs. Zere are European bankers even today with golden bricks numbering in the hundreds of millions smelted out of the sweat of my brethren's brow and out of their dental fillings. I think zere is still even a market today for tattoo lampshades. We should put one here. I can put it on during the cloudy days.... If I get ill, Shirl, or just wise up, you'll help me won't you?"

"You want to go kill yourself when there are a half dozen organizations that revere you, twenty or more students who depend on you, and numerous others who love you! No, Mr. Jacob Bruno, you leave me out of it! I'll tell you're 2 o'clock to come back tomorrow. Or next week." Shirley turned with resignation to depart, unconsciously tugging at her collar and rocking her head around to release hot air.

"And how will I pay za rent?" Jacob Bruno jumped to his feet. "Are you going to lend me za money! Give me five and send her in."

"Yes," she said, her customary smile returning, as the old warrior departed for his private bathroom.

Mrs. Theodore Titcomb strutted in, a lynx poised on spiked heels, wrapped in white sable, with her three carat bottom-kisser diamond ring, emerald studded cleavage, insignia engraved violet see-through stockings and darker pleated violet mini-skirt.

"Sit," Jacob Bruno suggested, as he stacked a recent case that had lain scattered in several sheets upon his desk. Mrs. Titcomb deftly lowered herself to the seat, flipped one leg over and displayed, apparently on purpose, a large portion of her magnificent thighs. The old man made no effort to hide his gaze as he watched her arch the raised foot and curl her toes back so as to dangle one shoe precariously.

A dog-eared text by her side, caught her eye. She placed it on her lap and read the German title *Handschrift und Charakter.* "Who is this Ludwig Kla-jeez?" she said, as she looked up to stare brazenly into the old man's eyes. Hers were glistening green. With long curled eyelashes, topped by pencil thin eyebrows, her face was capped by a perfectly crisp aquiline nose, lightly powered cheeks and supple lips painted magenta.

Mrs. Titcomb's tongue made a quick appearance as she waited for his response.

Bulging from his head like oversized grey olives, Jacob Bruno's eyes stared back. Saddled with deep bags underneath, these portals to Jacob's soul expressed a lifetime of experience in the numerous cry and laugh lines that surrounded them. Balding, but not bald, his wispy tufts of silver hair were brushed back over his rotund visage. "Klages," he corrected in his natural Austrian accent, "with a hard 'g.' "

"The book is dated 1928. And this one here," she lifted another well-worn text, "is it Saudek with a hard 'k'?"

Was she mocking him? he thought. "Correct," he said.

"Also 1928?"

"Yes."

"And here's another in 1926, by Osborne. Don't you have any modern texts, Dr. Bruno? Has nothing happened in your field in four score years?"

"Mister," Jacob corrected. "Zey call me Doctor, and I imagine I'm entitled to the appellation as I have two honorary degrees, but I never even completed college, it was..."

Marc J. Seifer
Kingston, RI

"Buchenwald, I know," Mister Bruno. I've read your file."

"File?" his eyes darted.

"Did I say file? Bio," she corrected.

"Oh, I see. Did you know that it was Klages that turned me in?"

"To the Gestapo!"

"Of course."

"This man!" she said, returning to the first text, holding it up with horror.

"Yes."

"And you keep his book?!"

"Books." Jacob Bruno guided her gaze to the jammed book shelves. "There you see his four major works. Like God, he cannot be explained. Za monster was an anti-Semite of the worst kind. 'Za Jew has stolen za soul of Germany,' he accused many times, but he turned me in not because of my religion..."

"Then why?"

"Because I was a professional threat!"

"He sent you to a concentration camp so Klages could be the only graphologist in town?!"

"Being Jewish didn't help. But, yes, and Klages sent many others as well, teachers, astrologers, palmists, philosophers.... My wife and son were taken, in part, because of Klages. This was before the war, when most often they only interned the head of the household, but he had them make an example of me and my kind. So, yes, I read his books, study them every day. Can you think of anything more absurd?"

"No, I cannot. Why would you ever do it?"

"Because, even after 80 years, za cretin remains za genius of our field. Quite a legacy. He's like a Freud or an Einstein. You cannot do without him. So no, to answer your question, the field has not changed very much since za dawn of the century. A handwriting is a handwriting, an analysis is an analysis, a comparison is a comparison."

Marc J. Seifer
Kingston, RI

"I'm ignorant, Doctor, er, Mister Bruno. This Klages book is about character analysis, is it not?"

"That is correct."

"And you study forgeries?"

"Yes."

"Are you a handwriting analyst or a detector of forgeries?"

"Both."

"Isn't handwriting analysis a fortune teller's trick?"

"Good day, Mrs. Titcomb." Jacob Bruno's manner changed rapidly. He turned his gaze to a large chained watch which he pulled from a vest pocket.

She paused to consider the fast rebuke; his peripheral vision caught sight of her full breasts heaving. Mrs. Titcomb was exceedingly beautiful, particularly her deep and entrancing crystal green eyes. *A superb nose job,* he thought, *slightly dimpled chin. Was that reconstruction too? Maybe her breasts were fake as well?* He hoped not. *If only I could see her handwriting,* he thought.

"That's it?!" she said, finally, breaking the silence.

"I'm too old and too tired to deal with another skeptic, Mrs. Titcomb," the ancient graphologue replied. "Do I look like a man who could spend his life wasting his time? We are what we write, so make up your mind. If I can be of help to you, I'm interested, but if you have your doubts, I von't be offended. Shirley can show you za yellow pages on your way out."

Jacob Bruno stood up and approached the women, placing a hand gently on her shoulder. His touch was warm, presenting it in such a way so as to leave the decision to her. A kindliness flowed from his fingertips as he felt, in return, zero response. It gave him a chill. Lack of love from the mother, he guessed to himself. Boldly, she placed her hand on his.

"I'm told you're the best."

"I am, Mrs. Titcomb."

"In forgery detection?"

"In every detection. You have a case?"

Marc J. Seifer
Kingston, RI

"It's my husband. He maybe having an affair." She reached into her purse. "I want to know if this is his." She handed him a one page letter.

"A love note?"

"So it seems."

Grabbing a magnifying glass the size of a pie plate, the analyst began to peruse the document as Mrs. Titcomb stared in fascination at the enlarged portion of Jacob Bruno's face. She was amazed to see a beehive arrangement of the skin cells on the tip of his nose. "To Monica," he said finally. "You know this girl?"

"By reputation only. She's a lady of independent means. Keeps four or five lovers who pay her rent. But I don't necessarily buy that my husband is involved. It was his son who gave me the note."

"From a previous marriage?"

"Yes, of course. I believe he wants me to divorce his father."

"So he'll get the inheritance?"

"What else is new. Can you do this? Can you match the letter to my husband's writing?" She gave him two copies of Theodore Titcomb's handwriting.

"Where are your husband's signatures?"

"Oh, are they missing?"

"They're not here. And I'll need the son's as well?"

"Is that important?"

"Well, Mrs. Titcomb, we have two questions here. Number 1, did your husband write za note; and Number 2, if didn't, did his son?"

"I'm not sure I can get the son's."

"I'll need the son's."

"I can't get the son's. Look, Mr. Bruno, I don't really care if it's the son's. I just want to know if it is my husband's."

"But, without the son's handwriting, you make much more work for me. Suppose they have the same basic style. That's often za case, you know."

"Because the son copies the father?"

"Partially, but also you have genetic components, inherited characteristics.

"But my husband's son was adopted," she lied.

"Oh, I see. Zat is a different matter. However, without the son's writing, this still increases the difficulty of the case."

"I'll see what I can do," she said.

"I will need an advance of $3,000, and if you want a written report, it will be at least an additional thousand."

"Your secretary said most cases run no more than a thousand."

"This is not most cases. If you get me za son's handwriting and some of Theodore's signatures, I can take off three, maybe five hundred dollars. Sleep on it, and if you decide, you can messenger the documents back to me with a check."

"I would want a detailed report, a precise explanation. Something to show my lawyer," she added.

"With charts and figures for each key letter?"

"Yes."

"Make it an even $5,000. And I must get it all up front."

"You will take a cashier's check?"

"A private check will be fine."

"I will send a cashier's check, Mr. Bruno. I can't afford to the time to wait for a check to clear. Time is of the essence," she added locking eyes onto his.

"I understand," he said returning her gaze.

"This is, of course, strictly confidential." Her eyes darted around the room, as she searched her purse for a mirror.

"As are all my cases."

Powdering her nose, eyes on the task, "May I leave the documents and forward the check by courier?"

"Certainly."

"For this kind of money, sir," eyes up to his, eyes back to the compact, " I expect a clear presentation."

"Chapter and verse." Jacob Bruno parroted the response she needed to hear. "Would you write me out a statement

Marc J. Seifer
Kingston, RI

agreeing to the fee and sign it?" He handed her pad and pen.

She hesitated. "Okay, Doctor," she erred on purpose.

"And, please, would you include your address. We needn't meet again," the Austrian added. "Courier is more efficient on my time, what little of it I have left."

"Are you ill?"

"Old. Eighty seven years is a very long time."

"You don't look a day over seventy-nine," she smiled, as she leaned forward to write out his request.

With his aging libido aroused, he accepted the note, and took her hand.

"Deal?"

"Deal." Slithering from her chair, she straightened her apparel and waddled towards the door.

"Mrs. Titcomb," he called after her. "You didn't give me your first name."

"Chastity," she breathed.

"Of course," he said as she closed the door behind her.

The old man dropped his eyes to the paper to stare at the artificial style which spelled out the agreement to the fee in measured fashion. Her address was a box number at Penn Station.

Maude Olsen
South Bristol, ME

Echoes

An hour ago this house was full:
Voices, laughter everywhere,
Bubbling noises filled the air,

Children shouting, crying,
Footsteps running to and fro.
Where did everybody go?

Now the sounds that were
Are bounding back from every wall,
    Fainter,
        Fainter,
            Like a ball losing its bounce.
Soon the stillness will scream at me
From every corner of this empty old house.

***

Nancy Galland
Stockton Springs, ME

Hadley Houses

Streets littered with fallen Spring
steal among moon-shadows of
tree limbs stretched over long
lawns, fingering old wooden
faces, looming pale in the light.
Death's dust lies heavy
in corners which once stirred
with the breath of farmers' feet.

Duane Brownfield
Chicago, IL

Echoes of Time

If you listen closely
You can hear the echoes of time.
The family vacations
The house you grew up in.
The close friends
And special relationships you shared.
The lessons your parents taught you,
And the values they instilled
That made you who you are.
The places and events
That changed your life.
The echoes of time
Make us realize
What's worth remembering.

***

Steve Troyanovich
Florence, NJ

hyperborean dawn

it is the quiet time.
drifting embers yet to be born.
over the hill: the first whispers
the darkness in oblivion's snow...

Stephanie Wang
Roslyn, NY

Chris Younger: Man-Boy

He is a man-boy—tall, wide-shouldered, blond scruff
like muddied hay on his head,
A thin patch of hairs already sweeps his upper lip.
His close-set eyes behind shadowy glasses
are curiously large and open.

He keeps his hands in hard fists.

I've seen him at school, sitting in the back of the classroom,
silent and brooding, blinking eyes staring widely at
the teacher.
He never takes notes, but
The teacher still smiles at him—a smile of understanding.

Younger never smiles.

Sometimes, he is made fun of for acting so much older,
duller.
Sometimes, in the streets right outside school,
I see him confronted.
He takes on three kids at once, fisting the jeering laughs
off their faces, knocking away the snickers and
threats.

I see him swing his arms, bear-like, as he towers
over them.
I see him walk away with his hands in his pockets,
disgusted.

Stephanie Wang
Roslyn, NY

He is so much different, so lost in the classroom.
        Yet, on the city bus home, as I see him brooding in
        his seat,
Leaning against the window and staring at the cement and
        graffiti outside,
        he begins to blend in.
I see exhaust seep into the wieldy public vehicle
As the doors swing open and disgorge a small stream of
        passengers.

The grey-black clouds cover everything in a fine layer of
dust:
A slate-colored dust of age and an unknown experience.

I look at my clean fingers, glance at his grey fists,
        and wonder.

William C. Davis
Fallen, NV

The Road West

Morning
Dove Creek Colorado
Sunny
Yet ancient and deserted
But a sunny road
A broad road West

Noon
Death Canyon Utah
Stark Mid-day
Lonely land/lonely road
A hot road West

Afternoon
Old Ely graveyard
Sad memories/faces dim
Getting late
A darkening trail
A trail West

Dusk
Ancient Austin Cemetery
Monuments/Emigrant ancestors
Ireland/England
They made the West

Darkness falling,sight fading
Can't read the names
It's trails end/in the West

Kristina J. Selting
Richfield, MN

Crossroads

Beyond the fury and willful madness—
what do we hear? When do the cries
of willful existence cease to voice
a noiseless wind? A moment ago; a
crossroads—you blink and here you are.
One voice, one mind-one heart-scarred
by anguish. Though it seems like
nothing—moments can take a toll. Was
it only your ear that was used, or
were you really listening? Can you hear
me? Looking through the hourglass—
eventually you'll see, our time is just
a speck—a myriad of moments, one true
kiss and then you're gone. Complacency
will steal away—time you try to store.
If it's important now—if it means
anything at all—don't wait. Are you
listening? Whether a matter of the heart
or your own row to hoe—Don't cast
aside the things that mean the most to you.

Dorothy Weiss
Orlando, FL

The Bridge

It is a cold brisk morning. My husband and I complete our usual physical exercise routine by walking around our neighborhood lake, and sit down to rest on a bench, observing the antics of swans, mallard ducks, and turtles. Suddenly from behind me, two black paws pounce on my back and a warm nose nuzzles the nape of my neck. Startled I turn around and face a black rottweiler, and an equally startled young woman trying to restrain him pulling on his leash. The animal is determined to get my attention. My husband, Monroe, quickly assesses the situation and laughs reassuring the woman and me that it is not an attack. For some reason, the dog wants to visit with us.

Monroe's own beloved dog, Larry, also a black rottweiller, had died years ago. He hadn't wanted another dog because Larry was so unique. But now he strokes this strange dog and talks to him gently. The young woman explains that she and her husband recently adopted the dog, from the Humane Society. He is a Hurricane Katrina survivor. His human "family" perished in that disaster. The dog managed to stay afloat in the floodwaters. I glance at him. He is quite comfortable with Monroe, but he keeps looking at me. "Okay, okay, come on fellow," I reach out, and he comes to me instantly, as if he recognizes a friend. I pat and stroke him. He plumps down next to me, leans against my knees as I rub him. He keeps nuzzling my hands. The woman is amazed, "It's the scent, he likes your hands." I chose to wear my mother's warm soft black knit gloves for warmth and inner comfort on that cold day. She had just passed away. She was 87 years. She had a full and joyous life. She loved lavender. Her gloves had a faint trace of that scent. The rottweiler sits quietly serene next to me. We both look out over the lake, seeing beyond the physical scenery, seeing something else, seeing someone

Dorothy Weiss
Orlando, FL

else, feeling comforted. I wonder if the family he lost resembled Monroe and me, and if a gentle kind elderly lady with silver-gray hair wearing soft knit lavender scented gloves had also been among those he lost in the storm. If only this dog could talk and share his experience, what a saga it must be.

Since then the rottweiler, Monroe, and I meet daily by the lake. His new human family is very understanding. They say he doesn't behave that way with anyone else. The dog looks for us, and when he sees us coming, the young woman releases him and he sprints to us. We hug him and pet him, and sit on the bench and gaze out over the lake toward that rainbow bridge in the heavens far far away. Someone is waiting there for us. Someone will greet us happily when we cross over that bridge. For now, we have found each other. We remember and love them. Life goes on.

***

Jeff Cannon
Worcester, MA

Old Fisherman by the Sea

In the waning hours of afternoon
The old fisherman exhausted by the morning's labors
Ignored the grief his body carried
And fought to find the attitude of youth

The sagging mound of beach upon which he sat
Grumbled under the burden of his dreaming
Tired fingers untangled weary threads of nets
Whose thousand salty eyes of oceans deep
Peered up at him with the glassy look of death
Powerless to temper his heroics

Jeff Cannon
Worcester, MA

They lingered about his feet
Not wanting to abandon him
While persistent winds of cool breezes urged them

They sought his touch
To massage once more their flimsy frame
Believing this time he would recognize the gift
Their seasoned hands scooped up for him

The old man wiped tiny pools of sweat
With a leathery hand from a leathery brow
And likewise wondered
About old urges and worn out habits
That no longer fed his hunger

Ancient passions flirted with him
But slight waves made them disappear
As they inched further up the beach
To wash his feet
At a distance dolphins quit their dancing
And kept a vigil

Pausing in the sunlight
That cooked away the flabby fat of dreams
The old man wrestled with the agony of urges
That would wrench him from untangling nets

Jeff Cannon
Worcester, MA

A mermaid came upon the beach
She brought a sea drink she especially made for him
He remembered her
She saved him once or twenty times
The old man thanked her, lifted up the cup and drank
And in the moment of the drinking
Let go the thought that would put him out to sea again

The old man with all his heart resumed untangling his nets
A tear slid down his cheek
Turning to wipe it away
He found the orphan boy from the village
kneeling next to him

The boy for hours, a lifetime
Knelt there just looking up to him
Waiting for the gaze of the old man's eyes
To recognize him and embrace him as his own

Catching the tear on the tip of his leathery finger
He placed it
In the boy's open hand for the lad to drink

Making room on the mound the old man said:
"Here my son, come sit with me.
Let me teach you about these nets and how to cast them.
Let me tell you about those eternal lessons
swirling in the currents of the sea,
filled with hungry sharks and dancing dolphins
and those mermaids who look out for fishermen
who don't forget to pray!"

Kenneth M. Austin
Redlands, CA

Obsession

I was surprised when Reverend Jones, a young African American minister phoned me about a Mrs. Carter he'd been seeing. Maybe it didn't bother him that I was Mexican because she was having thoughts of killing her twelve year old daughter. He feared she might hurt the girl and wanted me to treat her. Or maybe my race just didn't bother him.

Upon contact I found her appearance disheveled. Hair, black as pitch, uncombed, no make-up. "Can Reverend Jones come in too?"

"If you want."

With a deep voice the reverend presented her complaints and she began to cry.

"Why are you crying?" I asked softly.

"She—"

When he started to answer for her, I interrupted. "Reverend, please wait in the waiting room. I want to talk with Mrs. Carter alone. She'll be okay. You'll be right outside." I tossed him the biggest smile I could.

He seemed ambivalent, but stood and waited, maybe hoping she'd object. "That's fine, Reverend. I'm okay."

The door closed. "Mrs. Carter, I'm Dr. Alberto Gonzales, a psychologist. Please call me whatever you like. What should I call you?"

"Edith or Mrs. Carter is fine."

"Good. You were crying because?"

"I'm ashamed of my thoughts. I really don't want to hurt my girl."

"What's occurring," I said, taking a deep breath to ease my tension, "is called an obsession. What stimulates these thoughts?"

"When I see something sharp, like a knife or scissors."

Kenneth M. Austin
Redlands, CA

She hung her head.

"When I first see someone, I do a mental status examination and take a brief history," I said. "Let me ask a few questions. I'll make a few notes."

"I don't want any notes."

"But the law requires me to keep notes." *She's hiding something.*

My gut told me she wasn't a danger to herself or others but I asked anyway. "Have you ever hit your daughter?"

"Never, I wouldn't do that. I'm not that kind of person."

The exam showed depression but nothing else of significance. "Tell me about growing up."

"I'm an only child, born and raised on a farm. Both of my parents worked the farm."

"What about boys? When did you start dating?"

"I focused on chores and getting good grades, didn't date until I was working."

"Doing what?"

"Nursing. I was a surgical nurse...until these thoughts started." Her eyes watered.

"Sorry, but I need to know these things," I said. Wiggling in my chair a moment, I doodled.

It always helped me feel more comfortable when I doodled. "How old were then and what did you do about it?"

"I was thirty-five, about to be married. I transferred to the children's ward."

"Did that help?"

"Yes, I loved the children. Six months later I married and quit nursing. I was able to deal with things until five years ago when the obsessions started again."

"Have you ever been in a mental institution or had psychotherapy?"

"No, neither. Do you think I'm crazy? Can you help me?"

"You're not crazy, but I had to ask. I can help you help yourself. See you next Friday?"

***

Kenneth M. Austin
Redlands, CA

She slipped into my office, looking different. Her hair, black as a raven, was neatly combed. She was wearing make-up and was more dressed-up than when first seen.

"Hello, Doctor," she said in a near whisper, and sat slowly in a chair near my desk.

"Good afternoon," I said. "Are you feeling better today?"

"Yes," she said, her voice barely audible.

" Good, any incidents in the past two days?"

"Yes, I can picture myself stabbing my girl."

"You must hate her to want to stab her. What'd she do?"

Her voice went up an octave. "You're nuts! I love her. We've never argued." For fifteen minutes she bombarded me with all the good things about her girl.

"You can love someone," I said, "but be angry at their behavior."

"I'm not angry at her." She said in an angry voice.

I wasn't getting anywhere with my approach so I decided to breach her defensiveness in another way. "I'll accept that, if you'll think about it. It's difficult to think that someone can repeatedly think of stabbing a person they love, if they're not angry with them. Remember, I'm only asking you to think about the matter. See you next week." The door closed. I straightened the pictures of my family, sighed and completed my notes.

She was on time. "I couldn't think of any reason to be mad at my child."

"But," I said, "you're having images of stabbing her. This is an extremely hateful and aggressive thing. Why?"

I got a new tirade. In a hostile voice she said, "She thinks she knows it all. When she can't have her way she runs to her grandparents, turns them further against me. I've forbidden her from going there, but she ignores me."

She railed about her daughter for fifteen minutes, as if to justify her anger. Suddenly she seemed to realize what she'd been saying and began sobbing. "Oh my...I didn't know I felt

Kenneth M. Austin
Redlands, CA

this way. I'm a terrible person."

"Is that why you've had problems with your parents?"

"I don't want to talk about that. I'm leaving." She stood. "Do you want me back?"

"You're leaving early?"

"Of course, I'm mad. I don't have to stay."

"When do you want to meet?"

She fled as the words escaped her mouth, "Next Friday at two."

I reviewed her file. She was suffering a great deal from depression and obsessive thoughts. She needed relief soon. Then too, I believed she was extremely concerned with propriety and goodness. It would be difficult for her to reveal anything derogatory about herself. I had to get her to talk about her childhood.

After I rearranged the pictures on my desk, I relaxed a moment before finishing the day.

At her next appointment she was about to sit when I said, "What was different about the past week?"

She glared at me. "How did you know?"

She let her body plop into her chair. She paled, her skin turning white as snow on a sheet of tar.

"Tell me about it," I said as though I knew what she was talking about.

"A dream—over and over."

"Tell me the dream, please."

"My daughter ran away to my parents. But this time my husband went to pick her up. He took a belt to her and told her to stop running away."

"When she runs away are you the one that goes after her?"

"Yes."

"And you don't use a belt on her?"

"Never. How could you think such a thing?"

She glared at me. But I pushed on. "Has your husband

ever used a belt on her?"

"Absolutely not. I'd never let him."

"And your father," I asked. "Has he used a belt on her?"

Her tears began to run. "I don't think so." And then I knew her secret.

"But he used the belt on you when you ran away."

A sob hit her like a bolt of lightning. She gulped for air. She hung her head. Finally, she said, "He did it whenever I was bad—whenever I ran away."

"I want you to talk more about your relationship with your father but our time is up for today. Are you hiding anything else?"

"I never told anyone about his hitting me. He's my father, a good father. I'd never do anything to hurt him." I could see her body relax. *This was wonderful.*

"I understand. I think you may start feeling better now. Let's try going two weeks for your next appointment. You can always call if you need to come sooner."

After she left I adjusted the pictures on my desk once more and wrote my notes with new insight. I knew I'd dream a lot now.

She was ten minutes early for her next session. In a strong voice she started with, "I'm so happy. I've gone two weeks without any obsessions. I don't know how to thank you."

Immediately I said, "You could go back to nursing. A position in the children's ward."

Her hazel eyes widened in a startled look, much like a frightened deer. "But the obsessions..."

Calmly I said, "I don't understand your worry as that's unlikely. Besides, do you want to live life on a what if basis?" Talk to Reverend Jones, see what he thinks."

"Doctor Gonzales, what would you do and why?"

My eyes locked onto hers. "I'd put on my uniform. If it didn't fit, I'd buy a new one, and get back to what I enjoyed.

Kenneth M. Austin
Redlands, CA

You know I'll be here if you should need me."

When Mrs. Carter left I knew it was time for me to attend to my own dream. I shoved the pictures on my desk into a file cabinet. They'd stay there until I finished my therapy with Dr. Annette Dupre. I hadn't seen her in a year. It didn't matter that she was French. She was a good therapist and that's what I needed.

***

Anne Johnson Mullin
New Harbor, ME

After a Storm

Heavy snow bends spruce branches
so low they brush my shoulder, the touch
more gentle than expected, as if calibrated
to the merest feather of attention that makes me
look up through links of boughs and sky where
sun hits the top, the white dazzle then too much
to hold my gaze, which must back down
into shaded relief.

I think of Plato's parable, feel kinship
with the inmates of that cave, who retreated
into familiar shadows rather than stand
the jolt of too much light. I stumble if
I do not watch my feet on a winter woods path,
but looking up at intermittent brilliance
is worth a fall, worth every flash
of blindness.

Eve Gaal
La Quinta, CA

Overwhelming

The warmth of your love,
The touch of your hand,
The brush of very coarse stubble...
A squeeze,
Tight,
Like you mean it.

You are all that I could ever want.
A crude joke,
A fast prayer...
Your smile melts my heart every time.

Reading the morning paper,
Your eyes dance like music in my soul—
Your kiss warms me down to my toes—
I watch your serene face at church,
I watch your blonde lashes blink during a sad movie—
I listen to you snore into your pillow—
I hear you snipping bougainvillea in the garden,
Or making us coffee in the morning.

You're always thinking...
Or dreaming—
Most times about me...
How will you make me laugh?
Will I respond with a giggle
Or a sigh...
Will I cry?
Ahhhhhhhh....

Adrienne Butterfield
Winchester, TN

On My Mother's Death by Fire in Northern Indiana

Flat lands laid with an icy rime
Gleam now like silk in the sunrise.
Day wakens calmly, the countryside sleeps.
While over the farm fields a gentle wind,
Beseeched by a restless calling,
Quickens to Life in this quiet place,
Its own move impressed on the morning.

Fire birds blown to the wintry limbs
Hang now like crows in the branches.
Smoke rises slowly, a ghostly white shroud.
While under the rubble a gentle heart,
Possessed of an inner beauty,
Loses to Death in this lonely place,
Its own flame consumed by another.

Jim Andersen
Hermon, ME

Chance Encounter?

A True Story
In Memory of Lisa Carleton

Have you ever ended up somewhere you didn't expect to be; someplace you didn't even know existed. Maybe God guides our paths, lead us to places He wants us to be. Maybe there are forces that draw us to a certain place, at a certain time.

It was a cool day for this far south, at this time of year. Usually by Mother's Day weekend it's fairly warm in Southern Florida, but 65 with a breeze was not what my wife and I had flown down from Maine for. We were hoping for beach weather. Although the visit with my son in Fort Myers had been planned months ahead, his schedule still called for him to work the first few days we were there. So, we picked up a rental and went in search of a warm sunny beach.

Key West sounded good. We had never been there and were told the drive down was worth the trip. We hooked up with Interstate 75 headed south towards Naples. The South Florida traffic was a bit much for a Maine boy who was used to winding back roads. The only Interstate we have is 95 and there's not much traffic in the northern part of the state. The traffic got crazy as we neared Naples and I knew we would run into even worse traffic when we reached the East coast, around Fort Lauderdale and Miami.

My son told us if we headed south on State Highway 41 instead of following 75 east, we would avoid a lot of congestion and cut right through the Everglades. Highway 41 was a lot straighter and flatter than any road you would find in Maine at the end of mud season. There was almost no traffic and I settled into a relaxing drive on a country road.

This part of Florida is known for the Everglades and of course, alligators. We had taken many trips to Florida, but

Jim Andersen
Hermon, ME

had never seen an alligator in the wild. We were assured that if we drove this stretch of highway we would see some. As we traveled through the swampland, which should be teaming with wildlife, I told my wife, "Keep a lookout for the supposedly abundant reptiles."

"I always keep lookout," she replied. "I'm the one who spots moose along the roads in Maine."

"Okay, find us an alligator."

Thirty minutes into the trip we entered the Big Cypress National Preserve. Up until then we traveled through flat land that, although it looked a bit swampy to me, had been cleared for farming. Now the roadsides turned to real swamp, large cypress trees, low brush and a lot of water. Black stagnant-looking creeks crossed under the road every half mile or so. We stopped at several of these, but still couldn't find any of the elusive alligators. My wife spotted plenty of birds, mostly white egrets, and a big turtle that was trying to climb onto a log that was too small to hold him out of the water. He got part way up and the whole thing turned over spilling him back into the slime-covered depths. But still no alligators.

About half way across the preserve we stopped at the Visitor's Center. Beside the parking lot was a small pond enclosed by a fence with a sign that read, "Please Do Not Feed the Alligators." As far as I could see, there was nothing in the pond to feed.

We went inside the building, made out of cypress logs, to get some information. The lobby was filled with pictures of all the wildlife that you might encounter in the Big Cypress National Preserve, including pictures of alligators. They even had the skull of an alligator on a table in the corner and the skin of a ten-footer stretched across the wall.

I stepped up to the counter behind a man who had tourist written all over him. He was dressed in a flowered shirt that was almost as bright as his sunburn and shorts that ended just above his knee-high socks, which he wore with sandals. He removed his Boston Red Sox hat, wiped his bald head and with a heavy accent asked, “Where might I see an alligator?”

The woman in a ranger uniform laughed as though he had told a joke.

He looked indignant. “I’ve driven all the way up from Key West and haven’t seen any.”

“Do you know what a gator looks like?” She laughed again. Then she apologized. “I’m sorry. Sometimes when the weather is cold, they don’t come out to sun themselves until later in the day, but I’m sure if you continue along the road you’ll see plenty. Just stop every half mile or so and look around the stream banks.” Then she added, “But don’t go near them. They’re wild animals and they will bite.”

“What about the pond by the parking lot?” he asked.

“We no longer keep gators because we’d have to feed them and there are so many along the road, no one wants to see one in a cage.” As he turned to walk away, she added, “Good hunting.”

He mumbled something about southern hospitality as he left.

Ms. Uniform turned to me. “Can I help you?”

“No, um...no thank you. I’m all set,” and I left.

Ten miles down the road, and still no alligators, we entered the Everglades National Park. This piece of road is bordered by the park on the south side and a canal on the north side. The canal was dug to help control the water level of the everglades during times of drought or hurricane. The water level in the canal is controlled by water gates or dams every several miles. The dirt that was excavated from the canal was pushed up to form a bank along the north side, but unfortunately it blocks the view of the Everglades on that side.

Maybe it was because I was on vacation, but for some reason, alligators didn’t seem all that important anymore. We were getting closer to the east coast and I was now looking

Jim Andersen
Hermon, ME

forward to the Keys. Maybe we could see a shark.

As with a lot of things, when you quit looking, you find what you're looking for. I noticed it first, but it looked to me like the tread of a truck tire that had been thrown into the canal.

"There's one!" yelled my wife, pointing.

And it was a big one. It was lying on the bank on the far side of the canal. I stopped the car and we piled out with the camera. It was too far away for a good picture. I looked up the canal and noticed a water gate a hundred yards up.

"Lets go," I said, indicating the access road that crossed the dam. We drove across and walked the hundred yards back to the prehistoric looking beast.

My wife stopped a hundred feet from the eight-foot gator.

"Come on," I motioned to her. "We can get a closer picture than this."

"You heard what the ranger said. They bite and you don't know how fast they can move," she argued.

"Well, I'm going to get closer. Take my picture."

I moved to within thirty feet of the gator. "That's close enough," she warned and took a picture.

The gator hadn't moved. I picked up an empty beer can and tossed it at the animal. As I did, I took a step back. I won't say I was scared. I was just being cautious. It didn't even blink as the can bounced off its back.

My wife yelled, "Stop that. Let's go. I don't want a picture of it biting your leg off."

I stepped away and she yelled, "Look out!"

The alligator made a surprisingly quick, twisting turn and disappeared into the black water. We walked back to the car.

My wife climbed in on her side and as I started to get in something happened. It would make a nice story to say that I heard a voice or even felt a breeze blow across my face, but that's not the way it happened. I just looked up and saw a wide path going up the bank.

Jim Andersen
Hermon, ME

"Let's go up and take a look," I said. "We should get a good view of the glades from up there."

"I'll sit in the car," she answered.

I walked up the slope to the top. The Everglades stretched out in front of me as far as I could see, but that's not what made my breath catch in my throat. The path led to a triangular formation of stones that pointed out toward the Everglades. Even though I didn't know it existed and wasn't sure of my exact location, I somehow knew what this was.

I don't know how long I stood there overcome with a mixed sense of loss and pity.

I was suddenly aware of my wife walking up beside me. "When you didn't come back, I got worried and came up to see what you were doing. Are you okay?" She looked at the stones. "What is this?"

"It's a monument."

"To what?" she asked.

"Do you remember awhile back I told you a young woman I used to work with died in a plane crash?" Then it stuck me, hard. "What's the date today?"

"The tenth...no wait, it's the eleventh. Why?"

"It was on May 11th, 1996 that flight 592 burst into flames and crashed into the Everglades, right out there." My hands began to shake as I thought about it. "They all died, 109 people."

My wife took my hand and we stood for a long time, looking out across the vast sea of swamp grass or was it across a sea of time.

"Did you know this was here?" she asked.

"No."

"Then how did you find it?"

"I don't know."

Jim Andersen
Hermon, ME

Stones

Silent gray stones
with names and dates
representing the lives
of those before us.
Passage of time,
number of breathes taken,
If they could whisper
but one word,
The stories they could tell,
bleeding, healing,
crying, laughing,
hating, loving,
losing, gaining,
tearing down, building up,
each influencing others.
Each facing their final
unavoidable destiny
and laid to rest in peace.
If but one person
remembers their name,
and places a flower
on hallowed ground.
They will live on
forever.

Two days later, on the way back from Key West, I stopped at a secluded spot in the Florida Everglades and placed some flowers on a stone monument.

Mollie Schmidt
Rome, ME

Lake Blizzard

One ominous February afternoon
I ski our lake to meet the storm,
south end a blank of white but
north the pines still clear,
waiting for the steely sky
to lose its load. I slide
a hard and shiny surface,
skipoles prick and jab bare ice,
pushing into a rising wind—

then it comes, a spotted gust
of driven flakes blown level
with the lake, and now
I cannot see the trees, the bank,
my warm house waiting me
behind a polkadot curtain.
Awkwardly I step my skis around,
careful not to do a sideways split,
put up my hood to catch the force
that sails me home.

My tracks, not yet quite covered,
lead me back to the familiar shore,
the stand of whited, great white pines.
Gratefully I hug my skis and clamber
up the rocks, then see the swing
left out to sway in winter winds below
the largest pine—and why not
drop the skis and seat myself
upon the snowy plank and push?
I gather snow in mouth and hood,
a-swing out in the gale but safe
in the storm in my own front yard.

Meredith Shapiro
Roslyn, NY

The Midnight Walk

I looked out my window last night,
out towards the spiraling stars,
I could almost feel the wind outside.

There I saw the abandoned streets,
The once light yellow pavement in the front,
was now grey, basking in the dusk.

I looked out my window and amidst the darkness I saw
your face.

I decided then I'd take a walk,
Maybe my quick step against the quiet breeze would shake
the memories of you out of
my body.
Perhaps the cold would take the warmth out of your bitter
sweet touch.
Perhaps I could leave the confinements of my room
Maybe it was the walls that were enclosing the pain.

I tip-toed towards the back door, each step inaudible to
those asleep.
I reached for the bronze round knob, letting its smoothness
sink into the creases of my
hands,
Slowly I twisted my body through the miniature crack I had
made,
and once outside, I let the air envelop me
With its electrifying coldness stretching from my finger tips
to the rest of my body.

Meredith Shapiro
Roslyn, NY

I sank barefoot into the damp ground,
Letting myself drift down to the awakening dew.
Noiselessly I looked at the midnight sky,
With its yellow moon gleaming down at me.
It was then that my heart stood still, forgetting why I came,
I laid my head on the bed of grass and dreamt of tomorrow.

***

Mollie Schmidt
Rome, ME

Spring Garden

Blackfly bite behind my ear
and I know I'm in Maine.

Kneeling to plant alyssum, I
reflect on seventy-seven-year-old knees,

knobby fingers digging gravel
left in the bed by snowshovel.

Still, the colors are flagrant,
the wafting scent fragrant,

the satisfaction keen when all
the little annuals nod in their place;

I rub this aching back and find
myself still growing with the garden.

J. Donna Asmussen
Smithfield, ME

Vessel of Life

She sees me smile and thinks me
foolish. Do I not understand
the tragedy of life, the pain,
the uselessness? He sits in
quiet agreement, thinking
me raised in a sheltered
privilege, judging my life.

I look at him and cannot see
his heart, so cased and sealed to keep out
the fear, to keep in any small fulfillment of desire.

You will see someday, they say, in discomforted unity.
When you have the experience of loss, they say, only then
will you understand. You will no longer smile so freely to
the world.

Do I not understand loss, I wonder? What stuff of life has
touched me, passing through my life, moving on in time?
Desires and belongings, lovers and husbands, family and
friends. When we discover ourselves pots, do we not fill
our bellies with such things as were never meant to be
held within clay? Holding tighter and tighter as the
clay of our body ages and dries, finally breaking
apart as our body can no longer bear the weight
of our own desires? We will do anything to
stop the pain, the feeling of loss, anything
but see it as the true purpose of this
clay pot...to fill, carry, empty
and be ready once again.

Lena Moore Fleischhacker
Kalamazoo, MI

Pieces of Fire

"Herbert......Herbert......"

Mrs. McKenna, a plumpish, country-girl-pretty woman of thirty, was on her knees, her head bobbing about, scanning the underside of the old house. Like many dirt-road houses of the Georgia Piedmont, its silvery gray frame perched uneasily on four upright rocks; but, however uneasily, after seventy-five years, it still defied gravity, its underbelly hosting stray dogs, cats, chickens, snakes and generations of young children. It was one of several safe havens for Mrs. McKenna's fourth born, Herbert; and when Herbert came up missing, he was often located asquat and in a contemplative posture beneath the house.

"Huhbuht......Huhbuht......," in that neighborhood of Northeast Georgia, no "r's" in the pronunciation of the name, and often, "Huhbuht" became "Hub."

"Huhbuht......" Mrs. McKenna coaxed plaintively to the underside of the house, as if the boy would materialize upon her command, though his absence was highly visible. Upon which realization, Mrs. McKenna's vague sense of unrest turned into a full-blown panic attack, then and there in the year of our Lord, 1949, before the malady was tagged as a malady and joined the respectable ranks of the common cold.

The panic attack vaulted Mrs. McKenna upright in one unbroken movement, calling "Huhbuht," toward the peach orchard; then in the opposite direction toward Honeysuckle Creek; sent her circling the house to the back yard well, breathing relief when the well's cover was down, a sure sign that Herbert had not fallen into it; leaping up the back steps and crossing the sagging porch into the house to the kitchen, hoping that Herbert was asleep in the wood box behind the cook stove......she moaning between calls, "Lordamercy, where art thou?" as if Herbert would appear upon solicitation of his whereabouts. Which he did not.

With the last shred of hope that the child was somewhere about the house, Mrs. McKenna desperately searched the mildewed recesses of the dirty clothes closet for her big-headed, blue-eyed, curious boy of four.

When Herbert was not among the laundry, Mrs. McKenna knew she'd have to go beyond the house and yard to find him. But first, she went to the front room of the old house, where her fifth born, a babe of two named Avery, was sleeping and hauled him out of his crib, afraid that if she left him there, he, like Herbert, might come up missing.

With Avery locked protectively under one arm, she raced through the dogtrot hall, her panic escalating to a second stage, producing images of Herbert "snatched," as he played at the edge of the front yard. Where, in fact, she had seen him standing in the middle of her tiger lily bed, his chubby fist clinging to the bail of a blue speckled slop jar.

Of course. Herbert had walked up the road to the white oak tree to collect "frog money" from the red clay ditches of Copper Road. Again, a sense of relief.

Until panic, in its meanness, launched another assault; for Mrs. McKenna had a vision of Herbert at the white oak tree, dragged into the woods by a catamount, the one recently sighted in broad daylight. She was told that the beast, highly suspicious of humans, would not appear in daylight unless it was either rabid or ravenously hungry. Her heart pounding, Mrs. McKenna raced to the scene of the slaughter, where there was no sign of a struggle between a boy of four and a catamount.

"Huhbuht......Huhbuht......?"

And the woman was jolted by yet another shock of fear, remembering that just a week ago, her neighbor, Feather Crowfoot, who lived at the top of the hill, in the only other house on Copper Road, came to warn her. A convict had escaped the chain gang as they cleared the overgrown banks along the road.

"You keep yo eye out," the neighbor had warned. "Folks say he be hidin' in these woods......two-three folks done already seen 'im. One of 'em seen 'im sittin' up in a 'simmon tree wid a rock ready to drap on somebody's head......folks dat know, say the convict on duh chain gang fuh killin' somebody......"

Mrs. McKenna, a woman of unusually strong imagination, suffered another vision, this one of that murderous convict holding her Herbert hostage by the nape of the neck in one hand and a raised rock in the other. The sight was too vivid for mere mortal to bear; and still holding a bawling Avery more tightly, she staggered to the side of the road, collapsing into the ditch of cold red clay. And there, because the ditch had been recently cleaned by convicts, frog money sparkled like tiny pieces of fire. Trembling, she picked up several pieces of the mica-faced stones and studied them as if their glassy surfaces held the answer to some mystery.

A mile away on top of Copper Hill was a second silvery gray clapboard house; and inside, before a small fire, sat the woman, Feather Crowfoot, in a pressed back oak rocker with wide flat arms. Ely McPherson, her son-in-law, whom she disliked for marrying her only daughter, sat in an humble straight chair borrowed from the kitchen, where his wife, Lillian, did woman's work. It was midafternoon. Ely leaned forward, holding his pale leathery palms toward the fire.

"Reckon the rain 'bout stopped," he said to the little fire. "For awhile, anyway. If the sun stay out, it oughta be dry enough in the mawnin' to turn the high field. But wet as it is, ain't no way no mule be able to pull a plow in dat creek bottom. Reckon it'll wait."

"Uh huh," his mother-in-law agreed. "Dat bottom been theah sixty-two years, and if it ain't moved in sixty-two years, den it ain't goin' nowheah no time soon."

Lena Moore Fleischhacker
Kalamazoo, MI

"Sixty-two years!!!" Ely exclaimed. "How you come up wid dat? Dat bottom always been down theah, hundret years, two hundret years......don't nobody know......"

"If I told you onct," she interrupted him, "I told you a hundret times. My mama was a Indian, and she say the earth bohn the day a person bohn. I wuz bohn sixty-two years ago, and the bottom bohn same day as me." She paused stoically. "My mama was a Indian."

"Lawd help us," Ely said, and leaned toward the fire. Something tapped against the front porch wall. Ely bolted upright. "Dat fat little white boy heah again," referencing Herbert. "He ain't got no bi'ness here. I'm a mind to tek a stick to him or sic YapYap on him."

"How come you wanna sick the dog on Hub? What the chile evah done to you? He probably hungry again."

Ely McPherson argued, "If he hungry, how come he don't tell his own ma? Why he gotta come up heah, migh near a mile lookin' for food?"

Feather Crowfoot rose from her rocker, crossed the worn plank floor to the window and pulled back the curtain to look at Hub.

"He right pitiful lookin' wid dat ole slop jar. Evahwheah Hub go, dat slop jar go wid him. Come heah, look at him."

Ely kept his hands toward the fire. "Why am I gone git up from whut I'm doin' to look at him? I done seen him already wid his head big's a grown man's."

She accused Ely, "You ain't done nothin' all day long but hug dat lil piece of fire. Come heah and look. He got on over-haus three sizes too big and somebody done set a bowl on his head to mark where to cut his hair."

Ely grunted, "Huh."

"Who you sayin' 'huh' to? Don't you 'huh' me. Wutn't you taught you 'sposed to respect yo elders? I'm yo elder. I'm sixty-two years old. Now, git outn' dat chair and come heah and look at dat chile wid them overhaus cut off. Look like he got stove pipes on his legs."

Lena Moore Fleischhacker
Kalamazoo, MI

"Ain't nothin' to me," he replied, adding, "I wouldn't move outta dis chair to look if he was out theah buck nekkid."

And Feather Crowfoot shot back at him that, "Even if he wuz out theah buck nekkid, wid evahthin' he got showin', you wouldn't see nothin' no diffunt dan what you got."

Lillian, the self-appointed referee between the two warring factions, came into the room. Tall and thin, her skin reflected the light like black velvet.

"What y'all fussing about now? How come you cain't be in the same room without fussing with one another? Ely, ain't you got some plowing to do, nice and cool like it is?"

Two taps came in quick succession against the front of the house.

"And what's that noise?" Lillian asked. "Sounds like hail coming down. I can hear it all the way into the kitchen."

Ely shifted his weight in the straight chair. It's your friend, the fat, big-headed little white boy."

"Pore little thing must be hungry," Lillian said. "You reckon his mama even knows he's gone? She tells me she worries so much on account Hub comes up missing so often."

Ely said, "If I hear one mo rock hit my porch, he better come up missin' from my yard."

"I'll get him a biscuit," Lillian said, "and fill it with syrup. Hub likes sweet stuff." She went to the kitchen, and Ely's voice followed her.

"Dat's how come he heah......jus' like a stray dog. You want a stray dog to take up heah, give 'im sumpin' to eat and you got yoself a dog 'til the day dat dog die. Jus' like you got yoself a white boy wid a piss pot fulla rocks he chunkin' at my house."

"Yo house?" Feather Crowfoot asked. "My house. Me and Lillian, we live heah. You stay heah......"

A small missile struck the weather boarding.

And as if Ely himself had been hit with a rock, he jumped up, overturning the chair, which crashed loudly on the bare plank floor, collapsing in a heap of slats and rungs.

Lena Moore Fleischhacker
Kalamazoo, MI

"Dat's it," he said. "I ain't about to sit heah and wait 'til a winda gets busted."

Feather Crowfoot told him, "You the onliest one bustin' things. Heah you done got yoself so rile up over a little rock dat you done busted my bes' chair and Hub ain't busted nothin'."

"Chair wutn't nothin' but a piece of junk to start wid," he said; "but dis rung jus' what I'm needin'."

Louder and more urgently, Herbert hurled another stone against the front porch wall, just as Lillian reappeared with the biscuit.

Ely, at the front door, with the chair rung raised for battle, turned abruptly when Lillian spoke.

"You going out, Ely?" she asked in her quiet, un-demanding way. "Since you're going out anyway, take this biscuit to Hub." As she walked toward Ely, she explained, "I put extra syrup in it, so hold it easy so it don't leak on you and get you all sticky."

Ely, poised for the fight, looked at Lillian with an expression of confused disbelief.

"You tellin' me to tek him a biscuit in one hand and a stick in the other?"

"I ain't said nothing about a stick. Mama," she asked, "did you hear me say for Ely to take a stick?"

"Busted my bes' chair," Feather Crowfoot grumbled, and returned to the fireplace.

"I almost wish I was taking the biscuit to him, just to hear the way Hub says 'thank you,' " Lillian teased her husband. "His mama may not know where he's at, but she taught him good manners. Didn't she, Ely?" and smiling, she handed him the biscuit.

"He ain't gone be thankin' me 'cause I'm gone tek dat pot and throw it off down in the weeds. And den I'm gone show him dis stick so he know the nex' time he have a notion to thow rocks at my house...."

"You show talk big," Feather Crowfoot told Ely. "Mighty

big. I reckon you think you Samson goin' out theah to kill the giant. Whut you think dat chair rung is? You think that chair rung the jawbone of a ass? Look like the jawbone of the ass whut holdin' it."

Lillian held the door for Ely to go out, stick in one hand, biscuit in the other; then she went to the kitchen.

Feather Crowfoot gathered up the chair pieces and dropped them into the galvanized washtub where they kept the fireplace wood. Then, like a queen who'd won the throne, she settled into the pressed back rocker, folded her arms across her white apron and started to nod off.

A few minutes later, Ely, with chair rung in his hand, returned from his mission of defending the castle from the trespassing giant. He opened the door quietly, tiptoed across the plank floor and glanced at his mother-in-law, hoping the closed eyes and relaxed posture indicated sleep.

"You kill him? You kill dat big mean giant?" She was not asleep. "I hope you beat him good 'cause he's dangerous. No telling what Hub liable to do when ain't nobody lookin'."

Ely squatted before the almost no-fire. He pulled five flat, mica-faced rocks from his pocket and laid them on the brick hearth.

"Mama," he said, all fight having left him, "this is frog money to pay fuh the biscuit. I been instructed to tell Miss Lillian dat Hub is much obliged fuh dat biscuit."

"After he paid fuh the biscuit, den did you hit him up 'side the head?"

Ely McPherson held a piece of frog money in the palm of his hand and studied it as if its smooth surface held the answer to some mystery.

"I never harmed a hair on dat big head."

"Say what? Feather Crowfoot sat forward in the rocker. It ain't been ten minutes since you wuz standin' at the do wid a chair rung ready to kill 'im. Now I done seen it all. Ely

McPherson been outdone by a big-headed white boy ain't but fo years ole...."

"Well now," Ely defended himself, "I wutn't plannin' on killin' Hub. I was just fixin' to run him outta my yard, and theah I was across the porch, down to the bottom step wid the stick raised up, and here come YapYap, jumpin' between me and Hub, growlin' like if I tek one mo step, he gone sink his teeth in me......and I laid dat stick down and got myself back up to the front do 'cause my own dawg got his lip curled up showin' his teeth and hair standin' in a ridge on his back. I'm still holdin' the biscuit in one hand and my other hand on the do knob and I hear Hub say, 'I'm hungry.' "

"There he is, them blue eyes lookin' at me out'n dat big head, overhaus three sizes too big, and them ole wo out brogans wid no socks......shoes look like dey done walked a hundret miles......I've walked in dem shoes myself......sho have...."

"So," Feather Crowfoot smiled, "you give him the biscuit and he give you the rock?"

"By the time I give Hub the biscuit, I got syrup runnin' down my arm, and the biscuit flatter'n a batter cake. He broke it in half and give part to YapYap. Then......Lawd help us......he put the biscuit in the pot and his hand come out wid five pieces of frog money I'm 'sposed to give to Miss Lillian......Miss, he called her."

Feather Crowfoot spoke from the throne. "I'll say it again, then it's gone be jus' between me and you. You been outdone by Hub and your own dog. So, wheah dey at now?"

"After he count out the frog money, he took his pot and went up to the mailbox to wait for the school bus. YapYap followin' him lak he ain't never seen me, much less b'long to me. So I jus' set on the step and watch to see don't nothin' happen to him. Seem lak it ain't hardly no time befo the bus come and drap off the little boy and girl and dey all three went on down the hill."

"YapYap go wid 'em?" Feather Crowfoot asked.

Lena Moore Fleischhacker
Kalamazoo, MI

"No, he jus' go far as the top of the hill out theah, lak he makin' sure evahthin' alright. Den he come over to me waggin' his tail lak I'm the bes friend he evah had."

Ely McPherson stood up and took the broken chair rung, along with some strips of lightwood out of the washtub, criss-crossed them on top of the hot coals. The kindling sputtered, then burst into flames that broke apart into pieces of fire and danced up the black chimney, their light playing on Ely's face.

***

Hannah Fox Trowbridge
Harpswell, ME

Reunion

Two hundred six graduated years ago.
Back together again for brief hello's,
reconnects, later re-disconnects. Unfamiliar
faces with name tags bearing youthful images
strung around necks to dispel confusion.

Aha's echo throughout the gathering.
Recognition dawns like a clearing fog
as aged faces match teenage pictures.
Memories flood in as the years flash-fade
to make way for nostalgic reminiscing.

Too soon and not soon enough
the old tunes end, the clock strikes
twelve, classmates bid a fond farewell
to our once in a lifetime gig—
the 50th high school reunion.

Lesley Jane Briggin-Masuda
Santa Barbara, CA

News from the Front

The colonel reports from the front that losses are
unbelievably light.....
But I beg to differ......

What about the light that goes out in a mother's eyes when
she is told her only son is killed?

What about the light from the flame of the white candle
from the candlelight vigil......a flame which has been
snuffed out like the hopes for peace and compromise.....

What about the silver light of the desert moon, illuminating
a nightmarish landscape......the skeleton of a bombed out
barracks where U.S. soldiers lost their lives......

What about the light that explodes like a thousand suns in
front of a marine..........who will never see the sun
again.......

No, do not tell me the losses were light.......
For when one man falls, a star in heaven dies........
dimming the night sky........

Liz Moser
Baltimore, MD & Phippsburg, ME

New Widow

The first two weeks they hug you.
Your eyes tear up.
You smile and hug them back.
They tell you, oh how terrible, how
sad they are, how wonderful he was
before they walk away shaking their heads and dabbing
at their eyes with rumpled Kleenex tissues.

Hours pass. Full sun and rainbow-laden days, long
nights reaching out for warmth and substance for an arm
under the blankets, finding empty sheets and pillows
        unencumbered.

Next time you meet them all they say is "how's it going?"
They smile wanly and are on their way,
arms full of soap and lamb chops
from the supermarket, on their way to homes
with husbands sitting at the supper table
waiting to be served.

I need to touch.
I hunger in my fingers, in my elbows,
on my stomach and my back.
I lie in bed
breath caught unspoken moan
where are you why why aren't you here
I grab at pillows, any bulk to hold against my body
in our bed our home.
I should not be here by myself.
It is as though I am committing an indecency
when I try to find your warmth of skin and breath

(continued)

Liz Moser
Baltimore, MD & Phippsburg, ME

by switching on the old
electric blanket.

***

Cattails in Winter II

mourning the recent death of my husband

Today the field of other years
matches my mood:
setting sun silhouettes
blown heads shredded seed
frozen brittle stalks
no wind
quiet shadows on snow.

I don't look forward
to the greening. But
days will lengthen
drag me into mornings
I must master.

Chuck Murphy
Red Lodge, MT

Ladder

I do volunteer work at our local Boys and Girls Club here in Red Lodge. Mostly, I fix things. As a retired rancher, it's natural to fix things behind wild animals. This particular day the director wanted a banner put up against the ceiling above a window. The ceiling of that room is fourteen feet high. I have a twelve foot ladder so it would be no problem except that my family forbids me climbing ladders because I sometimes get vertigo.

But, the family wasn't there. I had brought the big ladder in and had one corner of the banner in place. I moved the ladder, climbed about seven steps and was reaching for the other corner. My vertigo hit. I hung solidly to the ladder and focused my eyes on the top as I started down. I prayed that I not fall, cause a problem, or disrupt anything. I wasn't fearful for myself. I just didn't want a scene.

When my foot hit the floor, a boy whom I didn't know said, "Let me do that."

I said, "That's okay. I just need to move the ladder."

"No. Let me do it. I'm lighter and I can do it."

"Okay." I handed him the hammer and tacks and he had the banner in place in no time. He helped me fold the ladder and carry it back to the pickup, then disappeared. I felt that I should pay him but something told me not to. I asked the supervisor if she had sent him to help me. She said, "No, Johnnie's just that way."

I know that God heard my prayer and told an angel, "Get in that kid and take care of that problem."

How long does it take God to answer a prayer? In that case, seven steps down a ladder.

Susan M. Murdoch
Milton, NH

Guiding Light

Oh, old faithful
friend of mine,
Over the turbulent
sea of time.

You are a beacon
of brightest light,
Who shines among us
each day and night.

Standing there proud,
tall and steadfast,
Beside the keeper
to the last.

A century plus two,
your story is true.
Inspire all who hear,
the call of the blue.

Faithful friend
to the young and old,
A guiding light,
you are to behold.

"Look up
and never down."
"Cherish each
new daybreak found."

Susan M. Murdoch
Milton, NH

From St. Croix
to Harbor light,
Over the seas
of foamy white.

You are our beloved
first lady of light,
You are the
lighthouse keeper's wife.

***

Maude Olsen
South Bristol, ME

River Light

The river light is softer
        when first I look to see,
Early in the morning
        before the world awakes,
Before the shadows scatter
        and bounce it all around;
Before the air is echoing
        with every sort of sound:
The dogs that bark,
        the boats that toot,
The dove that coos
        upon my roof.
All just before the day's begun, and then
Look out! Here comes the sun!

Caesar Valdes
Ashland, OR

Blossoms

I can hardly wait for springtime to begin
To see fruit trees show off their blossoms
With fragrance emitting from each limb
As rows of trees lined up like chorus girls.

Bees have performed their task beautifully
Pollinating as they buzz around each tree
And they provide a glee club so wonderfully
Synchronized with a harmony so very free.

As days go by the fruit begins to ripen on cue
Finally pickers climb ladders to extract them
Many busy hands pick rapidly leaving very few
So a fruitful harvest has now come to an end.

Reluctantly I watch this beautiful spring end
Wishing the year to hurry for another spring
Nature truly understands the art of recycling
Each year will bring a new crop to each limb.

John Hagan
Kettering, OH

A Frankenstein Night

The whole neighborhood abounds with local tales,
Haunted spots, and twilight superstitions; [...]
And the nightmare [...] seems to make it
The favorite scene of her gambols.
—The Legend of Sleepy Hollow
Washington Irving

Walking across a railroad trestle under a harvest moon at 10:45 was an adventure that seven-year-old Matty McGuire wished he had considered more carefully about a half-hour earlier when his two older brothers and three older cousins were making their clandestine break from the old farmhouse to the drive-in theatre down the road. Earlier that day he had eavesdropped on the five of them as they made plans in the saddle room to sneak out the window from a second-floor bedroom onto the bay window and down the adjacent trellis to watch one of the last movies of the season at the Stardust Drive-in Theatre. They had already tried to "ditch" Matty in the morning, but he knew from experience that their high-level caucuses were always held in the lean-to of the hay barn where his Uncle Joe kept the saddles and other tack for Dawn and Glory, the two Morgan horses that were as integral to Kerrigan family life as the three Border Collies were that shadowed the boys around the farm all day and slept in the spacious kitchen of the cavernous house all night. When the five older boys tried to make their escape around 10:15, Matty threatened to expose them if they didn't take him along. It was a crisp but comfortable Saturday night in mid-October, and Matty and his two brothers Sean and Danny had arrived Friday afternoon for another delightful sojourn at their Aunt Katy and Uncle Joe's sylvan paradise that would all-too-soon be consumed by urban sprawl.

Matty's Aunt Kathleen, or Aunt Katy as she was affectionately called, was one of his dad's seven siblings, and she had married the Irish farm boy Joe Kerrigan about three years before the bombing of Pearl Harbor. Aiden McGuire, Matty's dad, and Joe were both World War II veterans. Aiden, a captain in the Army Air Corps, had served as a ground support officer at B-17 bases, and Joe, a land-lover who had joined the Navy after the Japanese attack, had risen to petty officer first class by the war's end. A rangy 6'3" before enlistment, Joe's return to farm work had increased his musculature, but his frequent beer consumption had ballooned his girth. Many a summer evening would find him storming into the kitchen from the fields, popping the caps from two Blatz beers on a Coca-Cola bottle opener, and draining both brews in an eye-popping display of beer-chugging prowess.

At seven, Matty was six years his brother Sean's junior and four years his brother Danny's. His cousins Colin, Tommy, and Patty were twelve, eleven, and ten years old respectively, and they were three of Aunt Katy and Uncle Joe's four sons. Franky, the youngest, was only two, and each day he challenged the spindled sides of his playpen in the dooryard or kitchen, wearing a pee-soaked diaper in near perpetuity. While not the oldest of the group, Tommy at eleven was the inspirational leader of every venture into the forbidden zones, which included the gravel pit's lake, the Hereford bull's pasture, the house's widow walk, the grain silo's ladder, and the B & O Railroad's trestle. Tommy had not only tested and mastered them all, but he held the standing record for time spent (seventy-five seconds) in the field with Old Buster, the eighteen-hundred-pound mass of bovine muscle and semen that ruled his domain like an Egyptian Pharaoh, serviced Uncle Joe's feeder cows with a religious zeal, and dispatched bipedal intruders with an alarming alacrity.

The boys had traversed a bean field, a wood lot, and a cornfield before they reached the tractor path that ran next to the Mad River and the trestle that crossed it. They could easily have taken the dirt and gravel road that ran past the farm lane to the state route and then to the theatre about a mile further down, but that would have required more travel time and would have brought them to the front gate of the drive-in, preventing easy access to the "complimentary" seating behind the chain-link fence, just beyond the last row of cars and speakers. The dirt and gravel road was ambiguously named Prince Albert Drive, after either the austere Queen Victoria's husband or the popular pipe tobacco. The boys' unmarried and urbane Aunt Margaret, whom all the cousins called Aunt Maggie in her absence, often took the Greyhound bus to visit her sister Kathleen after a taxing week in the city as a legal secretary. She invariably glowered at the crusty driver on that route when he rudely and flamboyantly announced the Prince Albert Drive stop as "Tobacco Road!" Much like the oft-vexed British queen, Aunt Maggie was not amused. Matty had once overheard one of his teenaged cousins say that Aunt Maggie reminded her of the spinster whom Oliver Wendell Holmes describes in his playful poem "My Aunt."

Once on the trestle, Tommy led the way, followed by Sean, Colin, Patty, Danny, and Matty. The trestle was roughly a hundred yards long and spanned a shallow stretch of the Mad River. It provided a forty to fifty foot drop in the middle, and its crossties were gapped at about six to eight inches each. Whatever the spacing, Matty was convinced that one misstep would send him plunging through a gap to sudden death on the rocks or in the river below. In his excitement, however, he had taken about ten steps onto the trestle before his fears had taken control of his feet. By then, Tommy and the others, aided by the moonlight and plenty of practice, had bounded over the crossties out to about forty yards away. In spite of his daily irritations with his pesky little brother, Danny instinctively looked for Matty and saw him gripped in terror and staring down through the crossties.

"Come on, ya little fart! What're ya waitin' for?"

John Hagan
Kettering, OH

"I'm gonna fall through these boards!"

"No, you're not. Just watch your step and be careful."

"It's so high up here. I'm really scared!"

Either because he remembered his own trepidations during his first crossing or just because Matty seemed so vulnerable, Danny went back and coached his brother across the trestle. In the meantime, the others had bunched up at Tommy, who was irritated by the delay.

"I knew he'd hold us up."

Sean, struck by Patty's display of brotherly concern, offered his measure of sibling defense, "Shut up; they're comin'."

By the time these juvenile fugitives reached the rolling field of red clover adjacent to the grounds of the drive-in, the feature movie, *Frankenstein,* was well in-progress, a necessary development they had to accept if they were to avoid the parental detection that might result from a premature escape attempt from the farmhouse. Since all but Matty had seen the film at least once previously in an indoor theatre, no one was too disappointed by the late arrival. Typical of most drive-in theatres, the Stardust ran its coming attractions, short newsies, and color cartoons from 9:00 until about 10:30, so most of what the boys had missed was only the film's preamble to the fitful acts of the monster's savagery. Taking their seats in the clover, the five older boys buttoned up their coats and pulled up their collars. Matty mimicked their every move and feigned a blithe detachment as the Boris Karloff monster stampeded the clownish villagers and strangled his bug-eyed victims. Hours past his bedtime, Matty watched most of the movie fighting an oppressive drowsiness, but he knew that any request to leave would be met with merciless broadsides of "told-ya-sos" from the others.

As gathering clouds obscured the moon, the only ambient lighting emanated from the movie screen, and it flickered across the faces of the six escapees, causing a ghoulish result that rivaled the scariest scenes of the film. In the absence of speakers to provide diabolical dialogue, morose music, and eerie effects, the silence of the autumn night, pierced only by the esoteric discourse of two owls, made the black and white movie images seem all the more sinister. By the time the monster bellowed from the burning windmill at his pitchfork-wielding pursuers, Matty was so distressed by his gothic surroundings he wished he'd never heard of the Stardust Drive-in Theatre.

"Come-on," said Colin to the others as the movie credits began to roll. "We've gotta get our butts movin'."

"Do we have to cross that trestle again?" asked the mournful Matty.

"Well, we can't just fly across the river, can we?" said Tommy, whose own fatigue and anxieties were beginning to take their toll.

What Matty couldn't know was that the daunting railroad trestle would be the least of his fears before he awakened in the morning to one of Aunt Katy's sumptuous Sunday breakfasts, the aromas from which wafted up from the kitchen and beckoned the boys like Homeric sirens.

Arriving at the trestle, Matty looked upon it with a dread reserved for the most detestable of man-made or natural hazards. Given the late hour and the absence of the benevolent moonlight, all the boys now regarded the trestle as a kind of wooden-toothed beast that lay before them like a dragon lurking in a hostile forest.

Sean, recognizing Matty's understandable fears, said to the others, "You guys go ahead; I'll walk with Matty."

The other four started across much more apprehensively and carefully than they had earlier, and Sean stayed just behind Matty with a hand firmly on his little brother's shoulder. Since the crossing took much more time than anticipated, an unspoken but almost palpable fear began to engulf the boys. The elapsed time since their departure from the house was beginning to mount beyond their expectations, and the cloaking darkness was enveloping them like an atmospheric gelatin. Once across the trestle, they followed the paths between the cornrows rather easily, and they quickened their pace and gained a little time.

The Kerrigan boys knew that the wood lot would be even more of a challenge than the trestle, but if they picked their way carefully and stayed together, they should find the bean field quickly and be pretty much home free. Making better progress than even Colin thought they would, the situation seemed favorable until Patty said to the group, "Did'ya hear that?"

"Hear what?" asked the impatient Danny.

Everyone tuned his ears to hear what he hoped Patty had imagined. For a good thirty seconds, the boys heard nothing but their own breathing.

"Come-on," stage-whispered Tommy.

As they started forward, a voice broke the silence about fifty yards to their left, and as it rose in decibels, it raised goose bumps on all their arms, legs, necks, and backs. It lasted at least eight seconds before it died completely. In lung-stopping terror, the boys tried to divine the voice's exact location and identity.

Once more it screamed, now clearly the voice of a woman in horrendous agony or inestimable fear.

"Aaaiiieee. Aaaiiieee."

"Oh, no!" said Tommy, "It's the woman who was buried alive that Joshua told us about. Keep goin' or she'll rip our throats out."

Joshua was the ne'er-do-well loafer from down the road on Prince Albert Drive, who worked just enough for Joe Kerrigan to support a thriving whiskey habit and buy fuel for a Warm Morning stove that chased the chill from a three-room shanty. The boys knew he was little or no help to their father and that his pay was mostly a gift, but what he lacked in industry he replaced in folklore. He had once told the boys of a woman from the "farm over yonder" who, prior to the

Civil War, had been buried alive by her husband, claiming she had died from the Cholera. Everyone knew he was "meaner than a snake and crooked as a dog's hind leg," according to Joshua, so most folks in the vicinity just knew she wasn't dead when he buried her.

"Aaaiiieee. Aaaiiieee."

The cries now seemed almost next to the boys but remained baffling. Staying as close together as possible, the brothers and cousins navigated the remainder of the wood lot efficiently and set personal night-speed records for crossing the bean field. Tongue-paralyzing fear prevented even nervous chatter until they cleared the soybeans.

Only much later when the Kerrigan boys told their story of the alive-dead woman to their father did he tell them she was probably only a Red Fox that can sound almost like a woman in terror. Colin, Tommy, and Patty never shared that detail with their McGuire cousins.

Returning to the dooryard at 12:40, the boys were just about to begin their one-by-one climb up the trellis when the house lights came on and the kitchen door opened simultaneously. Onto the small porch stepped Uncle Joe, whose natural insouciance and affability were often disguised by his imposing height, his bloated beer belly, and his ham-like forearms. Aunt Katy stood in the doorway, silhouetted by the kitchen chandelier lights behind her. Uncle Joe spoke no words; he only signaled the boys with a jerk of his right thumb that meant to get into the kitchen, post haste. As the boys filed in, led by Tommy and Sean, Aunt Katy drew upon her best histrionics to effect a baleful stare.

"Where'ya been?" queried Uncle Joe, as if he didn't know.

"Drive-in," said Tommy, knowing he was the focal point of the inquisition.

"Whad'ya see?" asked the daunting father.

"Frankenstein," said Tommy, knowing his dad could care less.

During these preliminaries, Matty noticed that the razor

strap that had always loomed menacingly on a nail above the big cast iron sink in the kitchen was missing. He had heard tales of its punitive use, but he considered them more mythology than fact, until now. With this discovery, even his sleep-deprived dullness was no protection from the terror of what lay in the torments of the two-and-a-half feet of three-inch-wide leather that he now saw draped over one of the kitchen chairs. After some perfunctory exchanges with all the boys, Uncle Joe told them to line up a few feet from the bottom step of the long staircase and banister that rose gently from the expansive foyer up to a small landing and then a few more steps up to the second-floor hallway. Matty, who was always last in everything, was most pleased to be of such low station in this circumstance. Tommy, of course, was first in line, followed by Sean, Colin, Danny, Patty, and Matty.

"Grab your ankles," boomed Uncle Joe.

Whoosh, thwack, went the razor strap.

"Get to bed!" said the husky-voiced patriarch.

Tommy, who Matty decided had easily received the most potent swat, conducted a vigorous massage of his buttocks as he bee-lined up the stairs, but as a practiced recipient of these cowhide delights, he had stoically taken the leather without a whimper.

Sean was next, but unlike Tommy he had imposed no monk-like rule of silence upon himself.

Whoosh, thwack, went the razor strap.

"Owww!" he bellowed, as he too sampled the balm of massage therapy between the foyer and the second floor.

Colin, Danny, and Patty took their purgatorial turns with mostly the same reactions, although once in the hallway upstairs, Patty made the absurd claim to the other four, "Didn't hurt."

Now it was Matty's turn, and he did his best with a quivering lip to bend his tiny bottom toward his towering tormentor like the five big boys had done before him. A quick study of the drill, he placed his hands on his ankles without

John Hagan
Kettering, OH

directive but cast a furtive glance at Aunt Katy, who was biting her lower lip to restrict the laughter that was threatening to take control of a beautifully freckled face framed by thick red hair, a bit disheveled now from time on the pillow.

"Are you sorry?" boomed the judge, jury, and executioner.

"Yesss!" came the quavering response from a throat so dry and strained it could barely blurt the word.

With that came a temperate swat on the rump that was meant to teach but not to hurt, coupled with the boisterous directive, "Now, get to bed, you little rascal!"

Up ran Matty to join the others who had not seen the mitigated ferocity so unlike that delivered by their implacable magistrate. They could only stand in absolute awe of the little fellow who had endured his corporal punishment with such a stiff upper lip.

"Did he whack ya hard?" asked the inquisitive Patty.

"Oh, yeah!" said the little trooper.

"Did it hurt a lot?" asked the now respectful Danny.

"Oh, yeah!" said the little Spartan.

All six boys repaired to their cots in three bedrooms and pondered the evening's events. The five older boys were pretty much in the mental unison that while the adventure was something of a Pyrrhic victory, the thrill of watching *Frankenstein* free of charge more than compensated for the tingling they continued to feel in their still-rosy rumps. Little Matty's pre-slumber reflections, however, were briefer and mixed. He reveled in the presumed bravery of his valiant response to the unspeakable pain, but he went to an uneasy sleep imagining a hideous monster and a ghastly specter chasing him across an endless railroad trestle into oblivion.

Years later as a senior in high school, Matty would draw upon Uncle Joe's humanity as empirical evidence of the truth in Portia's "The Quality of Mercy" speech, rendered in William Shakespeare's *The Merchant of Venice.* He envisioned his Aunt Katy as the eloquent Portia.

Kathy Moran
Camden, ME

Rita's 90th, as told by Rita

Helen's invited Grace and me up,
like she always does.
She's a good soul, Helen.
Lame, though.

We'll have salmon cakes.
Told her once they was good,
and we've had 'em ever since.

She opens a can of salmon,
messes it up with some cracker crumbs and eggs,
and fries it.
Sets it on a plate with one small potato.

She opens one of them small cans of string beans,
and we divide 'em,
three ways.

We don't much eat at Helen's.
One small salmon patty, one small potato,
three string beans.
We come home to eat.

She's a good soul, though.

Manny Fiori
San Francisco, CA

American Interstate

Necessity is the mother of
Invention, or so I've heard
The old ones say
I believe somewhere along
The way
They forgot to tell us, that
At the fork down
The road
Where the abyss that is desire
Meets the endless that is need
The insatiable wanting
Which is hunger

Is the sacrificial
Lamb of fate.

***

House of El

Is there in truth no beauty
Why do so many deign
To look away
Are not lies a fragile framework
Are they worth the maintenance
Expense and crew,
Does not the lie claim asylum
Within the Fortress that is truth.

Myrtle Russell
Jackson, TN

Unraveling

America the beautiful, unraveling at the seams
Unshakable nightmares supplant illusive dreams
I just lost my home; the factory's long gone.
And the smoke-free bar just sits empty.

Torrent waters swell in unwonted places
Earth warming polluted skies; sun dried peeling faces
Wildfires; toxic dumps; abandoned towns of little hope
And the magnolia doesn't know when to bloom.

Come to Jesus on Sunday, the day we feed his flock
The doors swing open around eleven o'clock
Preachers tripping, choirs dipping, deacons sipping
And the feds found a bomb in the ashes.

Budget cuts, balooning prices; crime undeniably does pay
Swarming prisons, bustling courtrooms; drug busts
everyday
Politicians lying, innocent dying, fewer jets flying
And the ship at the border just changed its name.

Now ole Hank and Babe, they swung like true champs
No enhancements in their makeshift camps
Players sampling, refs gambling, chicks scrambling,
And my lace-ups cost three hundred bucks.

Amber grains stoking cars; gas prices underhandedly fixed
Nerve pills too high; two guys just got hitched
Computer dates, children raped behind guarded gates,
And the tower became an inferno.

Myrtle Russell
Jackson, TN

Swollen bodies float south as I flee in my truck
Frantic souls cram the stadium, all praying for luck
Levees breaking, bridges shaking, leaders faking
And the check never came in the mail.

Three chaps in the park, slender one likes to run
Two sit licking ice cream, daydreaming of cyber fun
Diabetic at eight, mom and dad overweight
And the surgeon just cut off my good leg.

America the beautiful, in line for a tortuous fall
Greed-driven madness; handwriting on the stately wall
Greece; Rome; Humpty Dumpty; Cinderella: they all fell
And the food keeps making my tummy hurt.

***

Nancy Galland
Stockton Springs, ME

A Five Heron Day

Arriving at dawn,
first a flying line in the sky—
then circling closer to the shore,
they stroked suddenly upward,
reeling clear of the birch
centered in my window.

Great grey wings
fanned the air with
ancient, archetypal power:
clearing time like trees,
as if this dawn still
belonged to dinosaurs.

Ray Gilliland
Yellville, AR

Gauntlet

If I could
Hold the World
In my
Hand,

Would I
Close my fist
Or let it
Go?

If I could
Hold the Rose
Of Love,

Would I
Crush it
Or would I
Let it

Grow?

Harold S. van Doren
Honoka'a, HI

The Wish Book

Whenever I look back at my early teenage years, I feel like blushing. I was so ignorant about girls! I went to a boys' private school, so there were no girls around to get to know. Besides, I tended to be quite shy. My summer buddy, Wayne, was younger than I, and, if possible, even shyer. By the time we were teenagers, however, we were both keenly interested in girls. After comparing notes, we were surprised to find that neither of us had ever seen a naked woman, or even a picture of one.

"What do you think they look like, Wayne?"

"I really couldn't say. . . ."

Hmmm. Not much help here.

Besides knowing nothing about girls' anatomy, we knew even less about how they thought. We would go to Friday night record hops in the town hall, and sit by ourselves at one end of the dance floor, looking with yearning at the other end, where all the girls gathered in a tight group. We didn't know how to dance and we couldn't figure out how to begin a conversation with them. So, all we did was sit on the hard, oak chairs, listen to the records and watch for two or three hours. We kept hoping for the miracle that two girls would magically break out of the knot to come over and snuggle up to us. Maybe, they might even want to take us outside in the dark and give us a kiss.

Ohhhh! How do we get girls?

Unlike Wayne, at least in the summer I was lucky enough to have a girl living right next door to me—Mary Ellen. She was a critical year older than I was, but sometimes, we went fishing together down in the cove off a lobster boat or rode around on our bikes. I enjoyed being with her, but I never knew what to say. She did most of the talking. I wanted her to like me as much as I liked her but I didn't know how to

Harold S. van Doren
Honoka'a, HI

have this happen.

Her father was a minister, and one day, he was trying to start his old donkey water pump engine without success.

I had been watching and figured he had flooded it, and I saw a chance to get in his good graces, as well as impress Mary Ellen.

"I'll bet I can get it to run. Can I give it a try?" I offered.

"All right, go ahead, that's very kind of you," he replied. So, I opened the throttle, muckled onto the crank handle and spun it with all the enthusiasm my fifteen-year-old body could deliver. With a bang, it started and a fiery cloud of burning gasoline came belching out of the exhaust at nose level.

"Holy crap!" I yelped, jumping backwards. Immediately, I knew I had said exactly the wrong thing, but my social skills were not developed enough to deal adequately with this situation. Instead, I slunk off in disgrace. After brooding for a while, I decided that there was nothing for it but to go back and try to make things right with Mary Ellen's father. When I knocked on the door, the reverend himself opened it, but he did not greet me.

"I ahh . . . hmm . . . I uh, want, um, to apologize for what I said."

He drew himself up, regarded me severely, and intoned, "It is not I to whom you owe the apology."

Again, I found myself at a loss for words, so I retreated and didn't spend any more time at Mary Ellen's. But, at least I could still see her because Mary Ellen used to hang around our neighbor's house almost as much as I did. Maurice and Helen Barter were "summer parents" for both of us.

One afternoon, she and Helen had a Sears Roebuck catalogue open on the sofa in the living room and were talking about the male clothing models. I stayed out in the kitchen, with ears wide open.

"I think I like the tweedy type," murmured Mary.

"Oh, he's some cute!" agreed Helen.

I didn't have to look at the picture to know I wasn't "the tweedy type" and never would be. They kept on "oohing" and "ahhing" while I sat wishing that the world, Mary Ellen, and I were all a lot different. After she went home, I picked up the thick catalog and turned to the girls' clothing section. A slim brunette modeling jeans caught my eye.

"There's what I want, Helen," I pointed. She looked and pulled on her cigarette thoughtfully.

"So that's what you want," she said. "Do you want to cut that out and take it with you?" In a way I did, but in another way, it seemed senseless to tease myself with only a picture.

"No, thanks, I guess not," I said sadly. "I want the real thing."

Next afternoon, Mary Ellen and I were both back at the Barter's. I sat in one rocker, and she sat in the other while we watched Helen making supper. I noticed that Mary Ellen was wearing a nice pair of plaid shorts.

"What are you going to do tomorrow?" she asked.

"I dunno," I mumbled, still nursing hurt feelings. "Maybe I'll go take a look at Dennis' old truck. You don't want to come along, do you?"

"Mmmmmmm . . . . Sure!" she answered, smiling. "Let's go early. I'll meet you up there by eight." She breezed out the door just as Maurice came home from hauling.

"Who was that I just saw leave here?" he asked, grinning. "Boy, oh boy, if I was a young fella like you and had a girl right next door to me, don't you think I wouldn't be doin' somethin'!"

"Hmf, I guess you think you would, don't you?" Helen sniffed.

"We're going to go look at Dennis's old truck," I stated, trying to sound as if it made no difference to me at all.

Maurice washed up in the kitchen sink and then began to shave. From his mirror, he watched me, his blue eyes laughing.

Harold S. van Doren
Honoka'a, HI

"Oh, you're going to go look at the old truck, huh?" he asked, suggestively. I knew that if Helen hadn't been there, he would have teased me without mercy, but even so, I felt too embarrassed to be around him any longer.

"See you folks later," I said, abruptly starting for the door.

"What's your hurry?" asked Maurice, with a smirk.

"I dunno, I've got to . . . ." I faltered. "I've just got to go."

On my way home, I thought how nice it would be to have an older brother to tell me what I needed to know about girls. Maurice was always full of ideas but, somehow, I wasn't convinced they would work for me. I felt I needed to figure things out by myself. That night in bed, I wondered what I could say or do with Mary Ellen the next day. Maybe I would tell her I loved her, take her in my arms and kiss her. I imagined her saying that she didn't want "the tweedy type" after all. Then, she fluttered her pretty blue eyes and said, softly, "Let's get inside the truck . . . ."

Next morning, I overslept. When I looked at my watch, it was ten minutes to nine.

"Oh, no! Now, what do I do?" I asked myself. Outside, it was raining very hard and the dooryard was full of deep puddles.

"Darn! It's too late to go look at the truck with Mary Ellen, and I don't dare to go see her at her house. She would never want to come out in this rain, anyway," I reasoned.

Through the day, I moped around inside. By late afternoon, the sky began to show some breaks in the clouds and there was a pink glow in the west. I walked over the wet, tarred road under the dripping spruces to the Barter's. Maurice was sitting in the living room, reading the *Bangor Daily News*. He looked up with a knowing smile.

"Did you go see the truck?" he asked.

"No, it was raining really hard."

"Well, that's too bad," he said, mournfully. "There was a nice girl up there this morning. She said she waited over an hour for some boy to show up, but he never came. . . ."

Harold S. van Doren
Honoka'a, HI

"What?!"

"That's what she said, wasn't it Helen?" he asked, glancing at his wife for affirmation. Helen stifled a smile, looked down at her knitting then back up at me, accusingly.

"When she came over here, she was soaked from being out in that pouring rainstorm! It's a wonder she didn't catch herself a death of a cold!"

I trudged home, kicking stray rocks and myself, knowing that I had really lost my chance. Why hadn't I gone? What had ever made me believe she wouldn't be there, just because it was raining? For years afterwards, Maurice never let me forget it. But, I had learned two important things about girls—you don't keep them waiting, and you don't stand them up on a date. As for Mary Ellen, she married a Greek, someone who was definitely not "the tweedy type!"

***

Steve Troyanovich
Florence, NJ

Elizabeth

softly you move
wrapped in my dream
sleepily the full moon
drifts behind your eyes...

your warmth covers me
like a blanket of starlight
all the rainbows
of the world
tucked into your smile...

Diane Wood
Belfast, ME

A Gift Without Measure

He was my first, one of several to come—this old horse....
The big truck pulled up in front of our store and home and
As the back was opened....there he was...wild with fear..

He left the truck with speed and strength....with no regard
To those trying to control him—an old soul who had not
left
The farm for the last hundred years.....

My father...wanting to please me...but by his own
standards..
Had bartered with a produce farmer to bring this gift to me
for the summer
He was here for a season and not at all glad of the move....

I trembled as I watched the tension ripple beneath his
battered hide
He had lived a long hard life and now it has come to this...
Companion to a frightened child who could only cry.....

But Daddy expected great things from the two of us....
I to become a horsewoman and the old plow horse was
Just in the wrong field at the wrong time...Daddy didn't
care...

But I did—my eyes finally met those frightened orbs and
Then it struck—right in my gut—the connection—the
knowing....
What was this....time was gone .... Fear was gone. Now it
was respect....

Diane Wood
Belfast, ME

Too much for me to grasp—still crying—still trembling but
when had this
Experience moved from fright to a bold communication—to
a melding of minds...
In mere seconds I had entered an ageless place without
understanding any of it....

Summer begat a routine of togetherness—he would carry
me...
Along the beach—along wooded trails—always the two of us
The season was short and we were comfortable in our
roles...
I the horsewoman and he the wise old teacher.....

He did not like the gentle touch, the caress—it was
unfamiliar
But at times I could bury my face in his mane and we
would speak
For a lonely girl and a proud old horse these were gifts in
time..
Permitted moments—I was not to believe this love to be
mutual....

Then the dreaded day was here—the big farm truck came—
and he was gone....
The loss was crushing...I was alone in his field ...my heart
would break...
His energy lingered—there was an awareness of him—we
had joined....
In my early years I had entered the ageless place and been
touched by the spirit...

Rozell Caldwell
Brownsville, TN

Thunderstorm
5-2-08

The thunderstorm
That touched down
In our town

Cut off the power
Bent trees over the road
Scattered them on the ground

The thunderstorm
That touched down
In our town

Increased
The recession
That was goin' round

The thunderstorm
Damaged our homes
But our churches were left alone

When our power
Was finally restored
For miles around

All one could see
Were peaceful trees
Lying on the ground

Katy L. Perry
Hallowell, ME

Uncle Maury Left More Than Memories

Uncle Maury is gone. Before he left, however, he annually gathered his own, his adopted family and multitude of friends and tied them together with a cord of golden love. Uncle Maury was that sort of man.

Morris Stein was born of Jewish parents, probably from Russia. When he met widowed, Stella Marcus, he fell in love. Not only did he fall in love with Stella, he early fell in love with her three small children and without even a second thought adopted them and became the only father the trio knew. In the first few years of their life together the vine of familial devotion was apparent. Together Maury and Stella had a daughter, rounding the family out to an even number.

Just months after their daughter was bom, Stella fell dangerously ill. For the next three years Maury, Stella's older children, with help from family members, cared for her. Nothing was spared in their loving concern for the frail, wasting lady whose malady was such that she could not, in any way communicate with her loved ones. Perhaps it was during those turbulent months the bond of unity was cemented between Maury and his "acquired" family.

I met Uncle Maury once. That one time was enough to sense the great devotion this humble man had for his family and his faith. It was Uncle Maury who meticulously lead the prayers at the Passover Sedar. Intoning the Hebrew passages with ardent devotion it was apparent to me, though I did not understand a single word he was reading, that what was being read was far more than words. His delivery came straight from a heart filled with true conviction for the lessons being told. I did not need to know what he was reading. I listened and felt the love he cherished for his faith.

During the past year, Uncle Maury's health failed gradually but he was cared for with tenderness and devotion by the

Katy L. Perry
Hallowell, ME

four children he and Stella had raised. His passing left a great gap in the family circle but true to tradition the "kids" were determined to carry out the annual ceremony as if he was still at the head of the table with his glasses tilted just right for reading.

It was again my good fortune to sit at table while Robert read—not quite as impressively as his father had done. Children, grandchildren, nieces, nephews, brothers and visiting strangers—18 total—gathered around a cozy New York City apartment and shared prayers, food—and love. No tribute to the absent member of the family could have been more poignant.

Strange isn't it, how one meeting with a person makes such an impression? Only for a few brief hours was I in the presence of Uncle Maury. I've heard the story of his family over the years, listing to tales of his life to such an extent that I feel I know the man. What comes through—although no one had ever put the fact unashamedly in front of me—was that Morris Stein was a person you could depend on and respect. That's how I will always remember him. The fact is, I remember him almost daily. Whenever I look for a notice or paper on my bulletin board, I see the crisp one dollar bill with a large, black Hebrew word printed on it. Uncle Maury sent this to me (imagine—a goy!) three years ago at Passover. I will never be broke because I could not part with this gift. Never out of money—or out of respect for myself. This dear, Jewish man, cared enough about me after a single meeting, to remember me with a gift from himself and his Faith. I am rich!

Peggy F. Brown
Gray, ME

View of the Gull

I cannot fly, but only try
to escape the bounds of land
Humanity's blisters on my soles
thoughts drift to nature; here I stand

To fly away and have this day
on the top of Cadillac
To spread my wings and carry my things
in a pack upon my back

I start my journey, leave behind
all worries in the dust
A gorgeous summer day in Maine
all stressful thoughts are hushed

I soar along the twisted path
then reach my summit view
The sky above is crystal clear
the ocean, sapphire blue

I breathe in deep,
the peace now creeps
into my aching soul...

Seagull soars across the sky
it's view is heaven-lent
The sunshine glimmers in my mind
as I start my slow descent

Lilli Lee Buck
Bristol, VA

Abraham Lincoln's Dreams

"Mary, Mary, I dreamed I saw
Our boys again last night.
Willie and Eddie were in my arms,
And I hugged them very tight.

"Then they clambered down from off my knees
Onto the floor and played.
They hid behind the chair, the door,
And romped the livelong day.

"Then they grabbed my hands and told me,
'Father, do come along.
You will be coming with us,
And it won't be very long.'

"Then they disappeared from sight,
And I thought I heard an angel's song.
I awakened in the morning light.
Could there be something wrong?

"Mary, Mary, I dreamed last night
I was sailing on the sea.
I was sailing toward an unknown shore,
Which stretched ahead of me.

"I couldn't see where I was going,
And all was veiled in mist.
The wind was calm, the sea was still,
And black as the River Styx.

Lilli Lee Buck
Bristol, VA

"Mary, Mary, I dreamed last night
My mother came back to me.
She was clad in her tattered homespun dress,
The way she used to be.

"We were back in our old log cabin,
In the deep Kentucky woods.
She was cooking at the fireplace,
And oh! it smelled so good.

"Then my mother turned and looked at me,
Saying, 'Abe, I'll take you home.
It's been nearly forty years
Since you wandered off alone.'

"She opened her arms to hug me.
I ran to her embrace.
Her old shawl fell across my back.
Her tears fell on my face.

"Mary, Mary, I dreamed last night
I stood at the looking glass.
And in that mirror I could see
The future and the past.

"I saw myself so full of flesh,
As I stand before you here.
Beside me was a paler face.
I felt a pang of fear.

"Mary, Mary, I dreamed I went back
To New Salem, Illinois,
Where I went to seek my fortune,
When I was just a gangling boy.

Lilli Lee Buck
Bristol, VA

"It was there I loved Ann Rutledge,
And she promised to be my bride.
But I wept for months upon her grave,
When Ann fell ill and died.

"Mary, Mary, in New Salem town,
The cabins stood row on row.
I recalled the voices of many friends
From a long, long time ago.

"But the voices had fallen silent.
The streets were full of grass.
The cabins were deserted,
With their roofs caved in at last.

"I called her name out, 'Ann! Ann!'
From my heart's misery.
I glimpsed her for an instant.
She waved her hand to me.

"Mary, Mary, as I was praying
On my knees last night,
My whole life swept before me,
And I wondered if I'd done right.

"So many gallant men have died,
And still they die in agony,
So that I could save the Union,
And let the slaves go free.

"Mary, Mary I dreamed last night
I was walking through our home.
I heard a sobbing, weeping sound,
As I walked through the halls alone.

Lilli Lee Buck
Bristol, VA

"I saw soldiers at attention,
All around in the East Room.
A long, tall man lay on the bier.
The place was thick with gloom.

"Mary, Mary, let us hurry!
To the carriage let us go,
Or we'll be late to Ford's Theatre,
And maybe miss part of the show.

"There's a comedy that's playing,
And I want to relax tonight.
Then we'll ride along the riverside,
In the fragrant April moonlight."

***

Nancy B. Wilson
Bremen, ME

Live Music

in memoriam, Muriel Havenstein

I cry.
I cry, but not for you,
Muriel,
for you were joy,
and have no need of tears.
But you are gone, and so
I cry,
for me, and for the
stunning silence of your
now piano.

Byron Hoot
Wexford, PA

Coming Out

Three crows flying
In a row
As if
They were hawks
Riding the air currents.
I know how
That feels
When something
Beyond yourself
Naturally comes out.

***

Just This

Now, therefore, there
Is no condemnation
                                        The way
A tree takes in cold
And heat to leaf
In spring, color in fall
Taking in everything
To be seen
As the beauty it is.

S. H. Weimar
Northville, MI

Train Tracks

His small hand clasped in mine, Ian stared at the huge locomotive and tender on display at the City Museum. There it was in all its splendor—black, powerful and awe-inspiring with cow-catcher splayed out in front. I felt small as a toothpick beside it and could only imagine the hapless feeling of my nine-year-old son.

"Dad, I love trains, but they are scary, aren't they?"

"These old iron ones with cowcatchers do seem a little overpowering, even to me; I love the excitement of riding on them, though, as did your mom. In fact, Helen and I took one similar to this on our honeymoon. We went to California and your mom loved sleeping on the Pullman cars. She had the lower bunk and I had the upper. She said she felt so cozy and protected lying in bed and peeping out the curtain to watch new passengers alight with their luggage. And then the chug-chug-chug would begin and the train would start up. But the old steam engines aren't made anymore. Now they are streamlined and faster than ever."

At lunch the train conversation continued. "You know, Ian, I've been thinking it might be fun to buy a train set, one that whistles and has lots of tracks with villages and stop signs and loads of other accessories. Would you be interested, or does the thought of trains sort of frighten you?"

"Geez, Dad, that would be great! No, of course I wouldn't be frightened of a toy train. One of the boys at school has a great set and one time he invited a few of us over to see it. His dad set it up in the basement and they never take it down."

"Okay. In that case, what do you say we go looking around after we finish lunch. I don't know if I'm doing this for you or for me." He gave a little laugh and saw a merry glint in Ian's eyes he hadn't seen since Helen's death.

S. H. Weimar
Northville, MI

We visited Lionel's and other well-known train suppliers and had a difficult time deciding which one to purchase. Ian finally chose a replica of the steam engine...because that was the type his mother had ridden and loved.

This was to be a birthday gift and since Saturday was his birthday, we had all day to set up the tracks and get started with the train. I loved the excitement shining in Ian's face.

"Geez, Dad, this is just like the one in the museum. It's really cool! Now I've got to save my money for more track and all kinds of cars and stations and people."

And that is what Ian did. Somehow he found an old engineer's cap which he wore every time he played with the set. In no time, we had a couple of villages, an automatic gateman, all in metal, who opened the door to his shack and came out to wave his lighted lantern. Also, we soon had highway flashers to signal the approach of a train at a grading crossing. We had train stations, lamp-posts and little people. It became a realistic village and we played with it by the hour. We added more track and cars; the set took over the entire family room. We barely had room for two couches and TV.

About once or twice a month I took Ian to the museum to see the original and he was bug-eyed staring at the giant as I was.

"It looks like the light is an eye and seems to follow me." He said one day as he squeezed my hand tighter.

Sometimes on my lunch hour I dropped in to see old "iron horse." I would stare and wonder just how much coal was necessary to get up enough steam to reach a speed of fifty or sixty miles an hour. I studied the massive heavy wheels and thought of the power of that marvelous creation. *Old boy*, I said to myself, *you're becoming obsessed with that relic.*

Contrary to my thoughts that Ian might tire of the train set, he continued to enjoy it, and the two of us stayed up much too late at times. Then one night after Ian had gone to bed I continued to play with the set, pretending I was the

S. H. Weimar
Northville, MI

engineer and had all the power to run a huge engine like the one in the museum. Eventually sleep overcame me and I unplugged the set and fell asleep on the couch in the family room.

In the middle of the night I heard a train whistle and felt the throbbing of the engine of a massive train. It continued toward me and I began sweating profusely and my heart beat erratically. The noise of the train grew louder and louder and I could feel the heat and hear the hiss of the steam. I wanted to scream as the train came closer to me. Its wheels screeched. Dear God, dear God, help me, I kept repeating but too late for I suddenly felt the weight of the mighty engine on my chest.

I was dead, I thought. I awoke and turned on the light. What the heck! The train had been plugged back into the wall. I distinctly remembered having pulled the plug. Quietly I peered into Ian's room. He was sleeping soundly. My heart still pounding, I pulled the plug again, left the light on and eventually fell asleep.

The next morning when I showered, I noticed two fine red lines running across my chest—the width of the train tracks on the toy set. *This is ridiculous*, I thought; *this has nothing to do with my strange dream. I must have scratched myself.*

About a week later I had a similar experience and knew absolutely I had pulled the plug from the wall before falling asleep. This time the red lines ran a little deeper, as though the train was traveling over the same tracks on my chest. I felt angry. I was frustrated and puzzled. I began to visit the museum weekly and staring up at the old locomotive. *Yes*, I wanted to scream, *you are the father of the train in my house and you are responsible for its going out of control. Now stop this nonsense!*

The nightmares continued. I developed heart palpitations and I was becoming irritable. No longer would I sleep in the family room. However, even alone in my bedroom the train pursued me. The tracks on my chest were now very

S. H. Weimar
Northville, MI

deep, but I was too embarrassed to see the doctor. After all, how could I say to the doctor, "Those tracks are caused by a toy train passing over my body each night." I'd be in the loony bin—and maybe that was where I deserved to be.

I thought of getting rid of the set, but Ian was enjoying it so much he spent all his spare time playing with it as soon as his homework was finished. How could I spoil his fun.

In the meantime, my nightmares became more intense. I would feel the steam on my face, hear the throbbing of the engine, hear the whistle as it came closer, hear the ssshhh as it was about to stop and then chug-chug, choo-chooing as it started up again. The noise in my ears was unbearable as it came closer and finally crushed me with its enormous iron weight.

Then one night Ian tore into my bedroom screaming he 'd had a nightmare. He said the train had come into his bedroom and scared him so badly he nearly wet his bed.

"Dad, I can't go back to my room. Can I sleep with you? I even felt the wheels going over me."

Before I pulled back the covers to make room for him, I pulled up his pajama top and saw the tell-tale tracks of the train.

That did it! The next morning I yanked apart the train set and threw it in the rubbish before someone else got hurt.

"But, Dad," protested Ian, "that was just a bad dream I had. It won't happen again."

I stared at him. "I'm afraid Ian, we have been too occupied with the train. I promise to buy you something you'll enjoy every bit as much."

My visits to the museum ceased. I bought Ian a computer game which totally fascinated him. In fact, Ian and his friends are still into computer games and I'm sleeping much better. The lines on my chest have almost disappeared and my heart beats normally.

Ian will soon be having his twelfth birthday. Has it been

S. H. Weimar
Northville, MI

two years since the big train fiasco? Thank God that was over! Maybe more computer games were in order for his birthday this year and I could throw in a couple of DVD's.

Yesterday while having lunch, I overheard part of a discussion at an adjacent table. The discussion centered around diesel trains versus the old steam locomotive. My palpitations returned. Without finishing lunch, I left the restaurant.

Last night I began hearing a train whistle and it seemed to come closer and closer to me.

***

Kathy Moran
Camden, ME

The Grooming

I married first when I was ten,
wiser then.

Swore vows to a captive clothes pole
groom of solid wood,
tall, gray-suited, square.
Stole long, impassioned movie-star kisses,
and danced in the sun under filament veils.

I wonder,
down there in the field by the well
by the house by the sea,
do the birches still stand,
carved with our hearts, and our initials?

David Campbell
Cape Elizabeth, ME

Presidential Campaign, January, 2004

1

One winter green is nature's unnatural emerald,
the male mallard's elbowed neck and skull
that could cap a princely walking stick,
kaleidoscope outside the cylinder, glints of Oz,
gemstone embers sinking to soot
with the slightest turn.
                                        Farther north
it's off-black fir and spruce in sawtoothed copses,
lightproof voids in a simpled snowscape,
damask over ice-age-chamfered
elbowroom that might be Sweden.
Then a coast so Nordic
it could only be Maine.

2 Dennis Kucinich in Maine

High energy low in the polls, rally to rally
down the coastline, working the gap between
All politics is local, all wars are foreign.

Reportage was strictly local: gray ponytail
behind a camcorder, a mother shoestringing
for the Ellsworth news, coffeeshop to church hall—
Norman Rockwell's patchwork unities, demography's
whole cloth in teenage skintights, workmen's drab,
pensioners' wool.
                                Your grassroots held
through winter's attritions, held this edge
where jettisoned connections
foul the tideline of an unmoored nation.

David Campbell
Cape Elizabeth, ME

3

Mallards skid to a halt like skiers
shot from ski jumps, then compress
to curling stones on the harbor ice.
The freeze is deep. The moon's weight
cracks the coves and tilts up slabs
like Arctic wrecks. Is the buried tide
half in, half out this campaign season?
Candidates go fanning south from here.
They praise all towns except the one
they curse and court and save in sweet
redemptive daydreams: Circe's whited trough
that makes men swine, turns gold to base.

***

Steve Troyanovich
Florence, NJ

a moon for Elizabeth

gentle thoughts
of your
full eyes...
this midnight moon

Hugh Fox
East Lansing, MI

Kaddish

Dying every night now.
knocked out with all I can
take, surprised when morning
comes and the thunder-clouds
are circling up from Illinois and
Indiana, the pond in the backyard
overflowing, the sound of rain
beautifully insistent on the roof,
never thinking in terms of large
bites, cuts, slices of Time, but only
today's rosebuds, the magnolia
flowers already down, everything
around me except the dead squirrels
and rabbits on the roads, coming back
into being
again.

Vera Louch
St. Louis, MO

Traded Lives

Jeremy Weeks was short and slender. Years of drug and alcohol abuse caused him to lose most of his once muscular build as well as most of his teeth. After being in and out of drug therapy, Jeremy managed to stay drug free for a full year. His olive skin was no longer blotchy, and puffy looking from all the drugs in his system. The bags had all but disappeared from his eyes. Even his hair stopped falling out... so fast. He managed to get himself a part time job delivering newspapers and telephone books, while paying off his drug debts. Best of all, after a few years of being drug free, he had become a good husband and father to his twelve year old son Addison, and his six year old daughter Alice. It wasn't easy, but Jeremy paid off all of his drugs debts with one exception. No matter how much he paid the dope dealer, the man continuously charged high interest and late fees.

Late one night, Jeremy arrived home from a twelve step meeting when the dealer, Judson Douglas, accosted him on the family's front porch. Addison had been peeking out of the front room window, so he could open the door for his dad. At the sound of angry voices, Alice and her mother also peeked out of the window. They watched in horror, as Judson suddenly appeared on the porch behind Jeremy. They were clearly visible, arguing with the darkness of the street in the background. The only light came from the bright porch light.

"I paid you $150.00 this week, man," yelled Jeremy. His blue-gray eyes were wide with anger and fear. Judson, unsteady from the drugs in his system, started to answer, then with a look of surprise turning into a frown on his stubble-covered face, he literally growled, "Who you yellin' at, I'm gonna' teach you some respect! I don't care what you paid, *I* want money, now!" He suddenly pulled out a small pistol and shot Jeremy in the chest, killing him, instantly. Then he went through the dead man's pockets and took everything of value. Spitting on the dead man, the killer then started to walk away, when he realized that the man's family had seen everything. Flipping them the middle finger, Judson ran off, into the night.

By the time the police and ambulance arrived, mother and children were still in hysterics. Neighbors who had been watching from windows and doorways identified the murderer, and he was apprehended, quickly.

At the trial, a now sober Judson Douglas was sentenced to five years in prison for possession of illegal substances, and life in prison for first degree murder, with no chance of parole. It was during the trial that Addison began keeping a journal on the effect that dope and addicts had on his family's life.

The years passed quickly. The Weeks family relocated to another part of town and got on with their lives. Judson Douglas was tall, about forty pounds heavier than when he was sentenced, and now he sported a deep scar that ran from the top of his left eye to the bottom of his left cheek. Prison seemed to have taken a lot of the fight out of him. He'd already served five years of his sentence and was two years drug free. He had become a model prisoner. The only visitors he had during that time were his mother and sister. After his mother died, Judson's sister stopped coming because she had "too much work to do at home." No one else ever came to visit, not even the mother of his son, whom he hadn't seen since the boy was six years old.

He was surprised when, one afternoon, he had a visitor waiting to see him. The young man was short, slender with pretty olive skin, a thick head of hair (worn in a medium length afro) and piercing gray-brown eyes. He introduced himself as Alan Strong, a sophomore in high school. He explained that his Sociology class was to interview a prisoner and discuss what led him to his present situation. "Well, why not," shrugged Judson, "I'm not going no place."

Alan visited Judson twice a week, and the more he learned, the more Judson learned about himself. He learned that life was about more than money and that when you show concern for others, they show concern for you. There were no cameras, nor tape recorders, just the two men, a pen and notebook. Working on that school project helped develop a certain amount of friendship between the two men. When the report was completed, and graded, Alan brought it to the prison to show Judson. Removing the cover sheet bearing his name, he showed Judson the finished project and grade—A+. Looking over his copy, Judson gazed out of one of the windows of the prison's visitor's room. His mind seemed to be somewhere else as he watched the people arriving and leaving the prison grounds, while enjoying the warm spring day. He spoke almost dreamily to Alan, "Well, I guess I won't be seeing you anymore, now." Alan smiled.

He was quite a nice looking boy, with a face Judson seemed to recognize from the past. "Actually," he said, "I was hoping you'd let me keep visiting you. I've begun to think of you as more than just a school assignment." Indeed, Judson had begun to see the boy as a partial replacement for his own son, where ever he was. Alan had even started calling the older man, "Pops." He told Judson about his family. He told him about his younger sister Alice who was also an "A" student and their mother, who was hard working, raising the children alone. "My father died of a drug overdose, and that's all I'll say about him, for now," Alan said, giving Judson a strange look. For the next two years, Alan continued visiting Judson, even sending him a Father's Day card. After he graduated from high school, Alan continued visiting the older man, discussing plans for college.

One afternoon, Alan came to the prison for his final visit. Judson knew this day was coming, but he was still unprepared. "Maybe you'll keep in touch," he said, trying to fight back a tear in his right eye.

Vera Louch
St. Louis, MO

"That's my plan," said Alan, "At least, I hope you'll still want to hear from me when you hear what I have to say." Judson looked at him, as worry started to spread over his scarred face, then he tried to play it off.

"Don't tell me, you're really gay! HAHA!"

"Naw, man!" laughed Alan, "I'm being serious! Do you remember the charge that put you in here?" Judson frowned, his eyes emitting a hard, dagger-like stare in Alan's direction. "What does that have to do with you?" he asked, speaking slowly and quietly. "I was there," Alan answered. Noting the man's surprised look of disbelief, Alan continued, "First of all, my name is not Alan Strong, it's Addison Weeks. I was twelve years old when my sister, my mother and I watched you argue with my father over a drug debt. We even saw you shoot him. His name was Jeremy Weeks."

Judson was staring at the young man. He knew he'd recognized Addison even after five years. Indeed, if there was one thing that haunted Judson, it was the memory of that wide-eyed little boy and girl, staring at him the night of the shooting. Addison's voice jolted him back to the present. "At the trial, I thought about how you took my father's life, and how drugs had taken over your life. I figured a life sentence in prison would make you suffer almost the way we did. Then, if you were ever released, I would hunt you down and kill you. Judson grew angry, "So all this was just one big plan for revenge?!"

"Keep it down, warned the big, beefy guard at the door to the visitation room. Judson turned to face the window, with its view of people enjoying the sunshine. "Revenge was the original plan," explained Addison, calmly, "but then I remembered something Dad used to say, once he stopped getting high, and whenever I complained about anyone. He would say, 'You should walk around in the other fella's shoes or get inside his skin to see what makes him the way he is and what he's going through.' I figured before I went to jail for killing you, I'd try to see the kind of person you really were.

In a way, I did take a life, only I took it in place of my dad's life." After a few moments of silence, Addison said, "My mom heard about the good work you've done as a prison drug counselor. She's forgiven you although she doesn't want to talk to you. My sister doesn't remember much about that night."

Judson still had his back to Addison as the young man continued, "I'll be leaving for college next week, so I won't be visiting, but I'll write to you from school. I left the school's address in the office, but I'll understand if you don't write back. Good bye, *Pops*."

During this last speech from Addison, and after the young man left the room, Judson continued facing the window. He wasn't angry, he just wanted to hide the river of tears flowing down his wrinkled scarred cheeks. Addison couldn't have known that among the courtroom spectators sat Judson's girlfriend, holding their six year old son. The boy, Judson Jr., was more handsome than his father had been at that age. After six months with no visitors, Judson's mother told him that his girlfriend stopped using dope, and was now engaged to be married. "I guess that's what you wanted, since you never went to see the boy or take care of him," added his mother, a month before she died.

Great, thought Judson, *at the time, for a $200.00 debt, I lost my freedom, and my son. Plus, I still didn't get the rest of my money.* He had already been beaten up twice while trying to collect on jail house drug sales, before he decided to quit using dope. He shook the habit, but he couldn't shake the terrified look in those children's eyes, nor the eyes of his own son, who stared at him as though he were some stranger, not his dad.

The haunting stopped the day Addison came into his life. That night, as he lay on his cot thinking about Addison's visit, Judson realized that he too, had taken (or perhaps traded) another life, in return for that of his son.

Judson whispered to an unseen spirit, "Jeremy, you

Vera Louch
St. Louis, MO

overpaid me, man." Imagining a forgiving smile on Jeremy's face, Judson whispered, "Thank you for sharing your son with me. I'll never replace you, but, I'll try to be a good father." Judson went to sleep, thinking about his first letter to his "son" at college.

***

Nancy Galland
Stockton Springs, ME

Green Beans & Grandparents

Green beans and grandparents
share a second wind:
the bean patch, when young,
gives abundance with vigor.
When all the blooms and
fruitful purpose fade,
it rests. Then slowly,
blooms again. And just
as frost fringes the
grasses at its feet,
the bean patch gives again,
less vigorously,
but rejuvenated
for a short time.

Hannah Fox Trowbridge
Harpswell, ME

9/11, AFTER 7 YEARS

Every year the anniversary
comes and goes. Much is made
of the "it changes everything"
event. Like lemmings,
we all follow the official word.
And believe it.

Few question the details
that lie to my common sense
and sure knowledge that tells me
100-story buildings don't fall
straight down
in 10 seconds.

No head scratching on missing
engines, vaporized plane parts
in field and Pentagon lawn. Where's
the exhaustive examination of debris?
The authorities always do that, don't they?
But didn't. Like lemmings, we believe.

I count myself among the crazies
who don't believe the official spin.
I'd rather be the nut case
who follows the money,
military explosives, unscrambled Air
Force, insurance deals, secreted Bin Laden's.

Hannah Fox Trowbridge
Harpswell, ME

The truth lies buried with the dead
at the bottom of ground zero.
The truth festers hidden
in the conspirators' minds.
The truth was demolitioned
in the Twin Towers and Building 47.

The victims deserve better.

***

Anne Johnson Mullin
New Harbor, ME

Sonnet in Snow

Walking in winter woods we pause to note
the brook that barely moves, its icy throat
muffled with frosted leaves and twigs, pinespills
soddening in passage, narrowing its rills.

Whence: the word is both a question and
a way to speak of source. To understand
what hidden power maintains this tenuous flow
we must imagine warmth beneath the snow.

So even when the coldest shadows fall
and days are dark, and friends may suffer all
we think unjust, then let us think again
of source, its strength, its mystery, its small
but steady murmurs into spring, and call
upon resolve to quicken sluggish veins.

D. C. Scherer
Greenwood, ME

Marley's Walk

I woke up this morning and did my usual stuff. After awhile I thought about going for a walk, which is part of my usual stuff. I made my way over to Main Street, then to Giga's house. I barked at her door, but of course she wasn't home. I then decided to go on over to see the children. I made my way over to Spring Street, stopping to say hello to Barney the cat. Did you know Barney was a stray cat who came to the O'Donnell's barn last winter when it was so snowy and cold? He is a big yellow and white tomcat and he lives in the barn, hence the name Barney. But anyway, I made it to the children's center and barked at the door but no one heard me. I hung around for awhile and then decided I would take another route home. I walked for some time and I guess I must have gotten disoriented. I started getting really tired so I decided I would find a comfortable spot to rest. I laid down and I guess I must have fallen into a deep sleep. I dreamed I woke up standing in front of a big golden door. I barked and the door opened. I looked inside and saw a huge green field with a large pond off to the left. There were dogs of every kind imaginable there. Some were running through the field chasing each other and some were sleeping under large shade trees; and some were swimming in the cool pond. Every now and then I saw a human tossing a ball, frisbee, or stick to their dogs. However the humans never stayed long, but the dogs didn't seem to mind. They were happy to have this beautiful place to call home and they were very well taken care of. I stood there and thought about my family, whom I loved so dearly. Then I thought this must be the place where dogs go when they are at the end of their walk, so I turned around to go back. But there was nothing but black. It seemed very cold and a little frightening. I turned back to the golden door and paused to watch one more time. Then I

D. C. Scherer
Greenwood, ME

walked through. I felt reenergized and safe. I thought about the life I lived and was so proud of everything I did, and every life I touched. My walk was good!

***

Al Beck
Monroe City, MO

Critical Zone

Many school learning experiences
have betrayed human exuberance and
jeopardized nature's curiosity
with mental frills plus much poli-madness.

Edu-madness purges understanding;
defining intellect as memorized,
expendable unbendable details
with a focus on flawed profundity.

What could be a more demanding
aspect of education's apropos attitude
than an enthusiastic competent search
to find a critical zone of creative comfort.

Martha Stevens-David
Minot, ME

Chronology of Aging

I'm young, she said as she danced by
Graceful as a butterfly
And young she was the truth be told
For she was only six years old

I'm young, she said to one and all
As she danced her prom dress down the hall
And young she was the truth be known
The fifteen years had really flown

I'm young, she said at thirty-three
And what the years have done to me
The birth of babies one and two
One with brown eyes, one with blue

I'm young, she said but not so sure
As she softly closed the kitchen door
I'm forty-five and still quite thin
It just depends what clothes I'm in

I'm still quite young, she keeps repeating
But I've got to learn to control my eating
Fifty-five, it's not too bad
I wonder why I feel so sad

I'm not so old, she often thinks
As she washes dishes at the sink
It's not so old this sixty three
As she dances grandchildren on her knee

Martha Stevens-David
Minot, ME

I once was young, she said with grace
As she smoothes the wrinkles on her face
The years have flown I know not where
And ask me if I really care

She seemed so young, they all said
As they fluffed the pillows at her head
Tears fell down as they filed past
This look at her would be their last...

***

Sally Belenardo
Branford, CT

Moonlight Sonnet

Full moon, you climbed a brooding sky tonight
and cleared the gathered clouds below, to soar
above the pines grown close beside the door.
You rose unnoticed, till from heaven's height
you shone a ray toward my distracted sight,
and, as I rested, through the window bore
the sharply outlined brightness on the floor—
a faded remnant of the radiant light
that drew us near when shore and ocean wed,
a summer past. Upon the sparkling tide
quicksilver moments slipped and hours fled.
In shadows, only, could the dark abide,
and, drowned in love, imploring you to stay,
we kissed as though that held the dawn at bay.

Bill Tucker
Aurora, OH

The Charley-Horse Story

I never could figure out why Coach got more excited about the games than we did. It wasn't so much what he said or how he acted; it was the way he looked. He got a kind of spooky look. That's not the best word to describe it; but it was the same look he got when he led the choir at the Baptist church. Maybe it was a holy look more than spooky. Anyway you could tell he was plenty excited.

Not that we weren't excited. Man, I can't think of anything more exciting than getting ready for a football game unless it's just before the kickoff. Just before the kickoff is really way the hell and gone more exciting I guess, but it's really something in the dressing room, too. The guys don't know what to do with themselves they're so keyed up. Everybody comes at least an hour and a half before the game. Coach makes us eat early, nothing but some real dry, lean meat, a poached egg and toast and plain hot tea with nothing in it. That's so we'll all get through going to the bathroom early and not have to go just before the game.

If you think it's easy trying to stay away from the gym during that couple of hours between the time you eat and time to dress out, just try it sometime. Believe me, you just can't think of anything but getting down in the locker room and fooling around with the other guys and talking about the game. Especially when your dad keeps asking you about what kind of plays you think will be the best against this team and how much you're going to win by and your mother looks at you like it was the last time she'd ever see you alive. Even without that, it's practically impossible not to let the excitement drive you out of the house, and there just isn't any other place to be but the gym.

I guess the night we played Greenville was the spookiest or holiest or whatever it was that I'd ever seen Coach. He

Bill Tucker
Aurora, OH

was almost sick looking, he was so excited. Nobody ever said anything halfway smart alecky or dirty though. Coach was a very religious man and showed up every Sunday to sing in this loud, bellowing voice he has while he directed the choir at the First Baptist Church. He didn't like anything smart or dirty. The only thing he did like was that he would fart once in a while where you could hear him, and he would just say "excuse nature," smile, and then go on with what he was doing.

But when we played Greenville there wasn't any use thinking of any funny stuff around Coach. I hate to say it, since I was on the team myself, but this team wasn't the best we'd ever had. The year before, though, boy we'd had a team then. These two great ends of ours both decided to join the Army when they could have played another year. They didn't even finish high school. And four of the first string that could have played had to go because they were over eighteen. That didn't leave us with much because most of last year's first string graduated. I was the second heaviest guy on the team, and I weighed only a hundred and sixty-five.

But Greenville. They really had a big bunch of guys, and they looked pretty old to me. I watched them get off the bus the day before the game, and I joked about how old they looked. I told Ernie that they must not have a draft board in Greenville. He pointed out a guy that was pretty near bald headed.

Considering the material we had I don't think we put up such a bad showing. We'd won three out of five. The two we lost were to GCMA and Baton Rouge and they were both having good years. We hadn't played anybody like Greenville though. They hadn't lost a game and all the sportswriters picked them to win the state championship. I could see why when I watched them get off the bus. Five or six of them would go over two hundred easy. This bald headed guy was one the big ones.

Coach's brother was the reason he looked especially

spooky, I guess. He was the Greenville coach and younger than Coach, our coach, that is Jules Hegan. His brother's name was Franklin, I think. We had never lost a game to Greenville since Coach's brother started there. But they never had that kind of material before. Now that I think about it, it must have been worry along with the excitement that made Coach look the way he did. He was standing right there when they got off the bus. You wouldn't have had to see them, though. Not after what they did to Central High.

I had been working out all week in a sweat suit because I had a charley horse in my thigh and Coach wouldn't let me scrimmage. That was all right by me. You get over liking scrimmage so much after the first year and Coach lets you help out with the second string if you're a senior, or first string, and can't scrimmage. I hurt my shoulder once before and got to help out then, too.

I was sitting up on this high bench outside Coach's room down in the basement of the gym and Coach was working on this charley horse. The other guys were kidding around like they always do. Most of them were naked or had just their jocks on. Everybody had to check their own gear to see if they were missing lacings or had loose cleats or things like that in the game equipment. We had good stuff for the varsity games and Coach made us take care of it ourselves. There really wasn't much to do but get dressed and it was hard to keep still, because of the excitement. Talking about the game made it worse, and it would get so bad that every once in a while some guy or another would let out a whoop that he couldn't hold any longer. Maybe a couple of the fellows would spar around a little, slapping at each other. If they started to wrestle, Coach would go over and give them a withering look and they would stop and sit down and think they had just ruined their chances of getting to play, especially if they weren't on the first string. This one guy had a way of slapping you on the stomach with his open hand when you weren't looking. It didn't really hurt, but the way he did it, it

Bill Tucker
Aurora, OH

sounded like a canon. Coach didn't think this was so funny, especially just before a game, and this guy wouldn't do it if Coach was any where around. He did it to a couple of guys while I was sitting on the bench. I could tell by the way they hollered.

My charley horse was a very bad one, and Coach couldn't seem to decide whether to put jism on it or not. Jism is this brown greasy looking stuff that he uses, and it burns like fire when he first puts it on. After that it makes your leg all tight, and starts to feel good. Your leg will feel strong and springy with jism on it for three or four hours, but if you sweat a lot it will start to burn again and get pretty uncomfortable. It wasn't very cold outside and Coach just couldn't decide.

"How does it feel?" he asked me.

"It's okay, Coach," I said. "It wasn't a bad one anyway. It's been feeling pretty good for a couple of days."

"You want jism on it?"

"I don't think I really need it, Coach. I hardly felt it at all today. I ran good yesterday. Never felt it after I got limbered up." I'd rather not have it than have it. My leg was good and tight feeling without the jism.

Coach kneaded my thigh a couple more times, slapped it to show that that was all he could do for it, and went into his room to get the tape. He came back and started tearing off these pieces of two inch tape about eighteen inches long and sticking them to the edge of the bench. You really got the feeling that you're about to start a ball game when the coach starts taping your ankles. You can always tell a football player, at least a backfield man, by looking at his legs. You'll see that his ankles are shaved up to about where the calf begins. That's so that the tape won't pull the hair out when you strip it off after the game. The ankles will probably look stained because of the stuff they put on to keep the tape from blistering the skin. It's brown colored like the jism, but it's a liquid and smells like creosote.

Bill Tucker
Aurora, OH

I stuck my leg straight out and Coach put on the first piece of tape. He starts by taking a piece in both hands and putting the middle right under the instep. He leans against the two ends he has in his hands so that it will be good and tight and then smoothes it out on each side of your ankle. About six or seven pieces go right under your foot like that and straight up the ankle then he criss-crosses about six more pieces in back and in front. After that he puts a couple of layers over the top of the instep. When he gets through you couldn't twist your ankle if you wanted to.

Usually Coach will talk it up while he is working on my ankles. I'm quarterback and co-captain and he always starts pumping me up so that I'll be as ready as I can get by the time we go out to the field. The only thing he said the whole time was that we were going to wear white jerseys. What he meant by that was that Greenville was going to wear dark jerseys, probably blue which is our color too. Whenever a team wears colors anywhere close to ours we wear white jerseys. That's because I'm so near sighted I can't tell who's on my side past the line of scrimmage, unless there is a real contrast in jerseys. Before Coach figured this out it gave us a lot of trouble in one game. I do most of the passing and the other team intercepted a lot that night. That might sound conceited, me telling about the whole team having to change jerseys because I'm near sighted. Coaches do that all the time though. There's lots of guys that can't see a thing without glasses and plenty of them are backfield men who have to do the passing. Coach found out about changing jerseys from another coach who had the same problem.

Well, anyway, he wasn't talking it up and telling me how this team was tough, but not tough enough. That's the way he would go about it. He'd never say a team wasn't any good, or run it down in any way. He'd just start working on you, telling about how we'd have to really quit on him, or loaf, or not play heads-up ball to lose this one. Come to think of it, he never said anything about losing when he talked to you before a game, and he never talked about winning big. Now I can't remember just what he did say.

But he didn't say anything while he was working on my ankles right before that Greenville game. I hadn't seen him talking to Ernie either. Ernie played right tackle and was the other co-captain and he kept the guys in the line all keyed up during the game. Coach always gave the whole team a talk right before we left the gym, and, if we weren't doing too well, between the halves. But it didn't get to you like it did when he had you sitting up on that bench with nobody else around.

He waited so long after he'd finished my ankles to say anything that I was about to get down and start getting dressed. When he finally did say something, he seemed sort of subdued and had this real spooky look I was telling about.

"What did you think of that bunch of boys that got off the bus yesterday?" he asked, trying to smile but making it sound very serious in spite of himself. I wondered what he wanted me to say.

"They were sure big, Coach," I said and watched his face. There wasn't any change, and it didn't seem like he was going to say anything right away so I went on. "Biggest bunch of high school guys I ever saw."

I forgot about Coach for a minute and thought about the size of the bald headed guy that got off the bus. It came to me while I was sitting there that when they got out of the bus, I hadn't picked out this guy Phil Hinkle, who was an all-state fullback and weighed one-eighty. I'd seen his picture on the sports' page and I should have recognized him.

"I didn't see Hinkle get off the bus. He made the trip didn't he, Coach," I asked.

"You worried about Hinkle?" Coach asked, but not in this accusing way you'd expect. Just serious.

"Nah. Hinkle doesn't bother me, Coach. Wait until old Ernie gets a hold of him." My voice lacked confidence. What I said didn't change Coach's mood.

Bill Tucker
Aurora, OH

All the time we were talking I kept having the feeling that Coach was sort of confiding in me. Kind of getting confidential so he could tell me something he didn't want the other guys to hear, or even think. I guess that's why I finally said what I did to his next question, but now, looking back on it, I can't imagine why I ever did say it. I guess it was one of the dumbest things I ever did.

"What do you think about tonight's game, Red?" he asked. He was standing there not two feet away looking right into my face and not smiling or anything. When a guy's face looks like that, white around the mouth, and tired, and not wanting any joking, I figure you'd better tell the truth when he asks you a question.

"We don't have a prayer, Coach."

Boy, was I wrong. I've done some dumb things in my life, but nothing like that before. My dad would call it real bad judgment. I knew as soon as I said it, that there wouldn't even be any use getting dressed. I had started every ball game for two years, but this was one I wouldn't start.

Coach jumped back from me like I had hit him in the face.

"Wha—Why—" His face got paler than it already was. "I'll just be damned." And the look he gave me. Boy, I didn't think I could have deserved that, no matter what I had said to him.

He turned and walked away. It was all I could do to get down off the bench and when I got down I didn't know what to do. If he told the other guys what I had said, I might as well turn in my stuff and go out for tennis.

He didn't, though. All he did was keep from looking at me. I went ahead and got dressed but before the team left the gym to go out on the field for warm-ups he came over to me.

"Take that stuff off and get out of the gym," he said. Nobody else could hear him, the way he said it. He's not that kind of guy, to say something like that where everybody

Bill Tucker
Aurora, OH

could hear.

Well, that's why I'm sitting here taking the tape off my ankles. It's been almost an hour since everybody left the gym but I just can't seem to get excited about getting my street clothes on and going home. My folks are at the game. I can't think of anything to tell my dad when he asks me why I didn't show up.

About twenty minutes ago Fred Chilton came in with his nose all busted up. He told me that big, bald headed guy plays right tackle. That means he's against Fred who is our left guard. Coach sent him in so he could go on down to the infirmary and get his nose fixed. Fred said he got it in the third series of downs we had. In between, Greenville scored twice.

I was right, though. We didn't have a prayer. Fred said we were getting clobbered. Now, I have to go home and explain to my dad why I wasn't the starting quarterback; why I didn't get to play at all. I know coach won't ever say anything to him about it. So, if I really limp around, maybe he'll believe the bad-charley-horse story.

Franklin Marshall
Simsbury, CT

Epilogue

an open letter to my wife, Elizabeth

An unsuspected finding: a potential health disorder, examination that resulted in a removal to memory the suspense of unknowing, the tenseness of uncertainty, the crisis in contemplation of an otherwise clinical soundness, and thereafter: a report of haleness and self-image recovery.

With you I rejoiced, but in my mind a picture persisted that I could not dispel: Standing in the doorway to my writing-place you said: "I suffer a bruising headache, my body flags with the exhaustion attendant upon sleeplessness and I feel of a sudden so old." At that chilling moment, your utterance expressive of distemperature struck to the marrow of my being with a sadness beyond imagining, for I sensed that behind your admission waxed within yourself a suspicion of terminal malady, and I knew that whatever salvaging counsel I might summon would carry no weight.

So then my companion and champion over decades of nutrient life, I importune: Distract me from my themes of disease and mortality with a farrago of happier visions and listenings: Persuade me to recollections of rain, where the drops with their trailers of moisture streaked the windowpanes of a convalescence in childhood; read to me the poetry of water in carriage over cobbles in a stream bed that breaches the shadows of a fern-strong ravine; describe for me elements, campestral, like an acreage of timothy grass so tall that the spore-rich spikes would tickle above our knees were we venturesome of ingress in search of the juiciest stem, as was our practice in youthtime; speak to me of those soil-mellowing worms that your shovel exposes, when you prepare an interval for planting; divulge to me the odors of a seashore marsh, when the tide reaches its limit of recession and the salt flat, runnel-rived and glistening, distends like a

Franklin Marshall
Simsbury, CT

plane of black gelatin; speak to me of features peculiar to a landscape at equinox, like the shower-begotten muck and mire of the sportsfields, like puddles and forest fens, like those little stones at a meadow's edge that twinkle back into dawnlight, like mirrors of mica, dew-beholden speckles of silver; compose for me a roundelay of birdsongs, an aria of wind, a solo for sails, an improvisation of oars, as the boats slip past the channel markers into their berths along the quay; tell me about that remote time when our Earth was all smiles, when the fish jumped out of school, when cormorants squabbled over a catch, and the spruce-towered, bayward sloping foreside echoed with the laughter of otters, but now no more, leaving an accusatory Why.

Dear wife, my caretaker and guardian over far more than a generation, deflect my disquiet, lest it consumes me, with politicians—that dishonorable and dissembling coterie, craven in its surrender to the colonels of commerce and industry, whose greed and imprudence unbalance the scale of ecological justice and who, with omnigenous machines decapitate an entire mountaintop for ore and would hack to logging rubble irreplaceable assets of wilderness.

How thin the veneer of civilization, for under the overlay breed the brutish male members of a terrible species—the single component of the animal order that befouls its quarters and kills for the sheer pleasure of it, be the victims mister or beast.

Deter me from further study of animal torture in laboratories and cosmetics manufactories, where the same experiments done a hundred times over yield results untranslatable in terms of human utility. Derail me from a track that would lead to a confrontation with the despoilers of countryside, that I may during the time, which is left to me, experience a relative repose knowing how my protests against environmental defacement and pillage will be greeted with abrupt dismissal and a sneering contempt, reserved solely for the patrons of animal freedom, for the defenders of wetland and

Franklin Marshall
Simsbury, CT

woodland against encroachment.

Divert me! Speak to me of cosmic dramas, like stars and constellations and galaxies imploding and exploding on the illimitable stages of space! Then I shall counter with a drama of our own, which I see as contingent upon sequence: Should you predecease me, I feel that I would follow shortly thereafter, having neither will nor mechanical means to continue, or perhaps our survivors may find us lying together at the death of ourselves and the world.

***

Patrick T. Randolph
La Crosse, WI

Celebration in the Mist

Up on Flat Bone Ridge,
Indian Cemetery—
Silhouettes appear;

Old mist-like whispering ghosts—
Warriors celebrate the dawn!

Jean Lawrence
Waldoboro, ME

Fall's Last Splash of Color

They call you winterberries,
But to me you are fall's last breath of life—
A splash of red midst the rust brown leaves
And bare branches that line the roadway.
Your roots rest in swampy places
Close by the choke cherries, now empty clumps
Stripped bare by birds made drunk with their fermented
fruit.

Berries of beauty,
I want so much to fill my arms with your lush fruit
And bring your color into my home to brighten the
shortened hours
That bring darkness to my days.
I want to capture your beauty—to keep it for my own,
To salt it away for colder, duller days when the sun
disappears
And snow seems around the corner.

Beautiful berries,
Robert Frost reminds me that "Nothing gold can stay."
I must transfer this wisdom.
If I pick your heavily laden branches,
In a few short hours, your color will fade.
Only in your natural state, in out of the way places,
Knee deep in water, do you glow.
Taking your color will rob your ability
To shine and bring joy to all who pass.

Jean Lawrence
Waldoboro, ME

So, I stand back and view you from afar.
I clasp my hands to keep from the selfish act of
Grasping your branches and cutting short your moments of
glory.
Shine on, winterberry bushes.
Shine on with Nature's last gasp of life and color.
Soon the cold of November
Will bring the long sleep of winter.

***

Roslyn Morrill
Rockport, ME

Ode to My Chair

Silent
In the background
Setting in a space
Sometimes here or over there
Taking no particular position
Open, grounded,
Sagging and drooping
I fold down to you
In humble release.

Jane Bruce Ward
Spruce Head, ME

The Dancing Man

twirls down main street
and into town—turning one way,
then another—arms, outstretched,
head back, eyes closed,
endless smile:
supplicant dervish, he,
awaiting benediction—
moves to a melody
for his ears alone,
and a voice only he can hear.

He is not scary, this dancing man,
though pedestrians move from his orbit,
drivers in cars stare in amused disbelief,
roll their windows up,
disappear into cocooned anonymity behind the black-
glassed windows and
safety of their S.U.V's.

Hannah Lackoff
Little Rock, AR

Bones

After Ben died, Cammie had watched Lindsay Fifty at the playground, laughing with her friends. She sat in the shadows of the big oak tree in her hand me down clothes and drank in the sight of Lindsay Fifty in her shiny new jumper sequined with the evidence of Mr. and Mrs. Fifty's wealth, and she ached to be her. It was not that Lindsay Fifty was particularly pretty. She was not particularly smart, or even particularly interesting. She was, in fact, shallow, simple, and spoiled; an only child pampered by two caring but distant parents, obsessed with the superficialities of money and appearance.

But right then, it didn't matter. Starting that summer she had wanted to be Lindsay Fifty for the pure and simple reason that Lindsay Fifty was utterly and completely ordinary. Her life was simple, arranged, predetermined. It held no surprises. They weren't allowed.

While every day Lindsay Fifty giggled with her identical friends and went home to eat dinner with her parents, Cammie lived in silence. Her parents' tiny house, which had once been filled with light brighter than any of Lindsay Fifty's sequins, was now dark and silent. The shades were always pulled down tightly to the window pane, and there was no longer the sound of baby's laughter or Mother's singing. Ben, who had been better than any shiny dress, any number of silvery friends, was gone. He was her father's smile, her mother's reason to get up in the morning. And now Ben was dead, and Mother wouldn't come out of her bedroom. Father wouldn't come home from working until it was too dark to see. He refused to light a lantern, but would pull aside the curtains and sit all alone in the gloom and eat his dinner. Sometimes, Cammie would sneak out of bed to watch him. Once, he caught her; the full moon made her hair glow, giv-

Hannah Lackoff
Little Rock, AR

ing her away.

"Come here," he said. His voice was gravely and soft. Obediently, she came a little nearer.

"Closer," he beckoned to her. His features shone in the moonlight. His voice was a little louder, a little harsher. She took another step and suddenly he pushed his chair over and lunged at her—grabbing her up in his arms and holding her tight, burying his face in her moon-glowing hair and mumbling words she couldn't make out. She stayed completely still, unsure how to react. She was really too big to be picked up, and even when she was smaller her father rarely touched her. After a moment he put her down and pushed her away. His face was wet and it glistened sharply.

"I'm sorry," he whispered, and she didn't ask for what.

It was another year before she found the bones. It was a bright sunny day, and for the first time since Ben's death, she opened the kitchen curtains to the daylight. For the first time since Ben's death, the kitchen saw light stronger than moonlight, and it was not sure how to react. It showed the dust and grime, and the neglect of nearly two years of housework. Insects which had taken to enjoying discarded scraps in a peaceful dark ran for cover under the furniture and old food boxes which had piled up. For the first time since Ben's death, Cammie tied up her hair and picked up a mess.

Most of the boxes were empty. They were crates of wood or cardboard that had once held fresh fruit and vegetables. In a nondescript cardboard box towards the middle of the stack, Cammie found the bones. They were small and whitish, varying from the size of a fingernail to about a foot long. There was no skull. She started and flung the box away from her, spilling its contents out onto the dusty floor. The bones clattered loudly in the quiet room, and she heard her mother stirring in the locked master bedroom. She picked them up as quickly as she could, shoving the brittle sticks back into their paper coffin. She didn't know who they belonged to, and she was almost afraid to find out. She was sure Lindsay Fifty didn't find boxes of bones in her family's kitchen. It was not the first time she envied Lindsay Fifty's oblivious lifestyle, and it wouldn't be the last.

That night, she left the box of bones on the newly clean table for her father to see.

"Cammie." He was knocking on her door. It was dark, there was no moon. She hadn't been into the kitchen at night for months. But he was knocking.

"Cammie." He opened her door and came in, and for some reason she was absolutely terrified. No one besides her had been inside that room since the death of baby Ben.

Father sat on the edge of her bed and stared at her. She drew her legs up under the blanket and scooted as far away from him as possible.

"It's not what you think," he said. "Those aren't your brother's bones."

She didn't know whether or not to believe him, but in the end it didn't matter. Word somehow got out. Word always got out. Sooner or later, all her classmates knew that Cammie's little brother's bones were kept in a box in the kitchen. Sooner or later, everyone knew. But no one asked. They just stopped speaking to her, stopped speaking at her or around her, or even about her. The closest she got to the others was when she watched Lindsay Fifty and her friends talk in the yard. By the time school let out for the summer, Cammie had not seen her mother in two years. Her father came home from work even later, leaving his daughter alone in the company of a locked bedroom door and a lonely box of bones. Alone every night in the dark, Cammie dreamed of living the ignorant, uncomplicated life of Lindsay Fifty.

And then the circus came to town.

Mister Zimitri's Big Top Circus! was garish and disgusting. It was cheap and decadent, and people for miles around paid a dollar for the bigtop tent, and fifty cents for the sideshow. The sideshow. The parade of freaks. Overly bright sandwich boards told tales of the Sad Clown, the Invisible Woman, the Boneless Wonder, the Two-Headed Man. There were midgets, a Fat Lady, the Living Torso, the Wolf Boy, the Four-Legged Child—it seemed freaks from every part of the world had congregated in one place, earning fifty cents after fifty cents, enduring hungry eyes and grotesque insults. Cammie stole a dollar from her father to see it twice.

The tent was dank and humid, smelling of sweat and urine. Calliope music tinkled faintly in the background. The crowd pressed together, undulating as one towards the platform up front. Cammie watched in awe, barely blinking, as the Fat Lady waddled onstage and danced, her mammoth roles convoluting sickeningly over her skintight costume. The Wolf Boy, covered in fur, scampered around—first on all fours, then on two legs—barking like a dog. And the Boneless Wonder—a tall thin girl made of silver who tied her body in knots—she caught Cammie's eye and smiled at her, smiled in a way that suggested she knew all about the contents of the box, and in fact, those were her bones, and Father was only keeping them safe until she needed them again. For the finale, the midgets made a pyramid of their bodies, and the Two-Headed Man carried the Limbless Wonder out and placed him on the top. The Sad Clown cavorted around them, and the Limbless Wonder wobbled to and fro, grinning happily at the fascinated crowd, but Cammie was barely watching. She was thinking of the silver girl—the Boneless Wonder. She was thinking of her eyes and her smile.

She had to get out of the tent, had to get out of this claustrophobic prison. Her head swam and she felt nauseous, but she couldn't push her way back through the crowd—they were pushing against her towards the freaks—they were shouting at them—calling them names and throwing bottles and peanuts and spitting at their retreating figures. The world grew blurry and out of focus, and then suddenly she was out—taking great gasps of air and sunlight and trying to quiet her head and her stomach, but it was too much, and she vomited a messy pile next to the sideshow tent. Then she wandered a little ways away, to a place where the grass was still long, untrampled by eager feet. She sat down and took out her remaining fifty cents and looked at it. She couldn't go back in there, could she? In the end, she put the coins back in her pocket and lay down, letting the grass cover her body.

When she woke up, it was to the sound of a man's voice and the sight of a few pale stars far above her.

"Last call!" the voice was shouting, "Last show! This is your last chance to see Mister Zimitri's Big Top Circus! Hurry and get your tickets! Half price! Last call!"

Cammie sat up and saw the shadow of the carnival barker, his top hat making its shape bizarrely irregular. She traded the barker for a yellow paper ticket, and stepped inside the big-top tent. Where the freak's tent had been hot and humid, the big top was cool and arid. Above, trapeze artists whirled. Below, tigers jumped through hoops and elephants let people ride them. It was a magical, eerie world. The crowd tittered nervously, unsure if it was all right to laugh and cheer for something so strange and surreal. The Freaks had had a label—the crowd knew it was allowed, and even expected, for them to boo the parade. But Mister Zimitri's Big Top Circus! was unfamiliar territory.

Cammie sat without moving, even after the show was over and the rest of the crowd had left, her hand clutching the worn wooden seat beside her. She watched as the barker and two mimes began to sweep the ring in the middle smooth again, flattening the footprints and skid marks out of the sawdust and dirt. She walked outside and saw the four midgets from the freak show smoking cigarettes, their faces shining redly from the lit ends. The white tubes reminded

Hannah Lackoff
Little Rock, AR

her of bones, and she walked home quickly over the fields, arriving back even later than her father.

The next day she was there again, and the day after that. She had no more money, and so she stood outside the smaller tent, watching through the flap whenever anyone went in or out. It was hard to see, but not impossible. After a while, she got the idea to go around the back of the tent and watch the freaks when they entered and exited. They were between shows, and there was only one there. The Boneless Wonder. She had a can of silver paint and a brush, and was touching up the places the color had rubbed off. She looked up and caught Cammie's eyes again.

"C'mere kid." Her voice was surprisingly ordinary. She handed Cammie the paintbrush. "Give me a hand."

Cammie dipped the bristle delicately into the can, and ran the silver sheen over the Boneless Wonder's shoulders.

"I'm Cammie." she said.

"S'ree." said the silver girl. She closed her eyes and let Cammie paint her eyelids and the bridge of her nose.

"So what's your story?" Her beautiful green eyes sprung open so suddenly that Cammie fumbled and nearly dropped the paintbrush. An orb of silver fell to the ground, staining the grass below it.

"Your story," prompted S'ree. "Are you a freak too?"

"My father has a box of bones that belong to my brother." It came out in a rush. It was the first time she'd ever spoken it aloud. The paintbrush dripped onto her foot.

"How do you know?" It came from the Fat Lady. The freaks had formed a semi-circle behind her as she painted. "How do you know they aren't bones from a chicken or a dog?"

"I don't." said Cammie. The Fat Lady just nodded.

"I'm Minnie." she stuck out her hand. Cammie shook it. It was like shaking anyone else's hand, there was just more of it. She was no more freak than anyone else.

Hannah Lackoff
Little Rock, AR

For one night, she was normal again. For one night, she stopped wishing for the life of Lindsay Fifty. Lindsay Fifty would never have had a night like this. Lindsay Fifty didn't have a box of bones—but she also didn't have any real friends. She couldn't talk to the Wolf Boy and the Two-Headed Man, or paint the skin of a Boneless Wonder. She would never breath in the smoke from a midget's cigarette, or learn that the Invisible Woman was only shy, the Sad Clown just a little lonely. Lindsay Fifty would not have known what to do when introduced to a Living Torso.

"I'm Dave." he said. He didn't have a hand to shake, so she just nodded. When you're a girl with a box of bones in your kitchen, greeting a man with no limbs is not a challenge. And when your body is only a torso, a girl with a curious past is nothing so extraordinary.

***

Patrick T. Randolph
La Crosse, WI

Two Lovers, Two Carp

Young lovers laugh near
The pond's edge—two carp come in
Search of stale bread crumbs;

One lover's eyes looking down—
One carp's smile is pure human.

Cindy Partington
Dallas Center, IA

Beyond Touch

When your eternally silent presence arrives
and fosters kinship with the night,
you calm my trembling spirit.

Although the whirlwind puffs and swirls,
and its dust stings my eyes,
your remembered breath feathers my troubles away.

If sleet's arrows stab my face,
and my hands grow numb,
your distant warmth melts bad memories.

Whenever oppressive heat bakes my skin,
and my pores exude sweat,
your long gone elixir fleshes out the poisons in me.

As soon as spasmodic lightning flashes,
and rain clouds let loose,
your ever flowing words cleanse me of regret.

When I linger in darkness
and probe the future's mysteries,
your shadowy presence illumines the way.

Richard H. May
Goodyear, AZ

Blondie's Incredible Rescue Journey

When Germany surrendered in WWII, the U.S. Army southern division was deep into southern Germany. The scout division had been in the forefront of the heavy fighting since landing two days after D-Day. When the news of the surrender reached the troops, there was instant jubilation and shouts of joy. At last the worn out troops would be on their way home.

Sargent Jim was the leader of one of the veteran platoons. The platoon had lost many men, and the remaining men were close-knit friends. The division lieutenant ordered Sargent Jim to send six men in his platoon to scout for any German soldiers surrendering. Platoon Corporal Paul soon came across something which would cause great consternation to his sargent upon his return.

The scouts came upon a destroyed barn, probably from tank gun fire the day before, where Corporal Paul noticed a dead female boxer near the barn, and four baby puppies...which evidently had been birthed just before the mother died. Paul felt the four puppies; all were cold and dead except the fourth pup, who was warm and still alive. He picked the pup up and proceeded back to the sargent with it. He couldn't leave the helpless little puppy, which started to whimper in his hands.

A surprised Sargent Jim held the puppy in his left hand...where Paul had placed it. Jim, a large rugged man, was truly perplexed, in fact astounded! The puppy in his hand whimpered, and Jim realized it was hungry. He knew he couldn't let such a sweet little puppy die. But how to feed her. He had no bottle with a nipple. He sent Paul to get some canned milk. Jim had an idea—he would dip the little finger on his right hand into the can of milk and see if the puppy would suck the milk off his little finger. She sucked Jim's fin-

Richard H. May
Goodyear, AZ

ger at once. Jim held the pup in his left hand and continued dipping his finger until the puppy had enough and fell fast asleep.

Looking down at the little puppy asleep in his large left hand, Jim announced to his platoon that he was going to try and take the puppy home. The men thought he was crazy to disobey the general's order on allowing no pets. But they were a loyal bunch of battle-hardened friends, so they agreed to keep her a secret.

Jim liked the light color of the pup's coat, so he named her Blondie. That night, Jim lay on his back in a sleeping bag with the pup placed on his throat, under his left hand. This would keep her warm while Jim slept. Paul had emptied the water from Jim's canteen and had filled it with canned milk. When the pup whimpered for a meal that night, she woke Jim, and he immediately put the little finger of his right hand into the milk. It took a number of finger dippings to satisfy Blondie. Jim fell back to sleep in-between feedings when the pup also went back to sleep.

During the day Jim held Blondie in his left hand, who was placed down at the bottom of the large, deep pocket of his winter trench coat. His left hand kept Blondie warm. In time, Jim's left hand and throat became a wonderful substitute for the pup's dead mother.

The train trip to the French port took almost three weeks because of delays en route due to torn up tracks having to be replaced. In the meantime, Jim kept Blondie buried in the left pocket of his trench coat. It became her home.

When the platoon boarded the troop ship, Sargent Jim and Paul shared a compartment. While Paul held the puppy and fed it, Jim took his first shower in three weeks.

After leaving the ship in New York City, Jim and Paul were discharged from the Army and paid separation money. On the street, Jim hailed a taxi and was driven to the nearest vet, who checked Blondie over and found her to be in good health. The vet made a carrying sling that Jim could strap over his shoulder. It contained a nice pocket for the pup, and this allowed Jim to free his left hand. About this time, Blondie opened her pretty little eyes. It was a very moving experience for these two battle-hardened men to see such loving eyes looking at them.

The morning after leaving the ship, Jim and Paul went to Central Station in New York City to catch trains for home. Jim was catching a morning train to Chicago and then another to Seattle. Paul bought a ticket for a train to his home in North Carolina. Jim stood on the train platform next to the Pullman car where he had purchased a compartment ticket. Facing him stood his good friend Paul. When it was time for Jim and Blondie to board the Pullman, it was also time to say farewell to Paul. Paul reached into Jim's sling and withdrew Blondie. He brought Blondie up to his lips and kissed her. Jim noticed tears streaming down Paul's cheeks, because Paul knew he would never again see Blondie...a puppy he, as well as Jim, had fallen in love with.

The trip home on the train was a relief for Jim. No longer did he have to worry about the lieutenant discovering Blondie and destroying her. Also, the baby bottle with the nipple the vet had given him made feeding Blondie much easier. Additionally, on the train he had a source for fresh milk from the train steward. In a matter of a few days Jim arrived home to Seattle.

This story is true. I met Jim about a year after the war was over. I admired his beautiful 60 pound female boxer named Blondie and asked if he still slept with his dog. He smiled and answered, "Yes." He said she had her own pillow and her own side of the bed. His wife slept on one side, Jim in the middle, and Blondie on the other side. This is an example of a very understanding wife.

A couple of years later, my family and I moved after I took a job in another city. I never saw Jim and Blondie again.

After all these many years since this story happened, I

Richard H. May
Goodyear, AZ

never forgot Blondie; but I did forget Jim's last name. Now that you, the reader, have read about Blondie, I chance to say I doubt if you will ever forget her either.

***

Russell Crabtree
Rockland, ME

Frigid Pink

I remember a few regrettable occasions in
which I was on hand to witness bitterly cold
winter sunrises from a vantage point
overlooking Rockland Harbor: Sunlight so
devoid of warmth that it seemed to accentuate
and crystallize the intense cold,
illuminating the smokes that stood in columns
over the harbor with a frigid pink
luminescence. Chimneys expelled plumes that
looked like vertical contrails that hung
motionless in the still, arctic air. A scene
as barren and lifeless as a lunar landscape.

Sharon Lask Munson
Eugene, OR

Keeping Company

She lingers as I reflect
the seasons and years
stories into verse—
small events
snowflakes melting on my tongue,
skimming cream from bottle tops.

She's there watching as I stir
chicken fricassee
wings, drumsticks, some meatballs
flavored with onion, sweet paprika, and thyme.

She notices
as I observe the world
through wide eyes
teachers, politicians
soda jerks

and the butcher
who lays his index finger
on the scale and weighs in the balance
ground beef and grace.

Eve Forti
Bremen, ME

Thanksgiving

Glassy-eyed, gutted, they hang
from a neighbor's maple tree
where months earlier
sweet syrup ran
and weeks earlier
a child's green swing rocked
in a sudden breeze.

In autumn deer provide
a feast for him and food
for thought reminding me
of cycles and struggles,
how quickly things can change.
Reminding me I'm far from spring,
still hungry for life.

Linda Hewitt
Lincolnville, ME

Opium

I caught the scent before I saw her...that heavy, spicy, almost cloying scent of Opium. My close friend in California wears only Opium by Yves St. Laurent, so I can always identify it. I bought some for myself, but it just doesn't smell the same on me. I do wear it in the winter when the spirit moves me and I'm trying to create a sultry, dramatic aura. It is a fragrance that retains its potency for hours, and it cannot be confused with any other. And it seems to somehow change according to the body chemistry, and perhaps the personality, of its wearer.

She came from behind me in the supermarket parking lot, the scent of Opium preceding her. I was admiring huge pots of hardy chrysanthemums in so many vibrant shades, joyful sentinels of the coming fall season. I had purchased two pots of bright yellow mums the week before, and I was debating whether to buy two of the rust colored ones for my new stone patio. At only $3.99 per plant, they were hard to resist. As we both stood together, admiring the beautiful colors and smelling the peppery and pervasive aroma of the mums, I remarked how beautiful they were. She smiled up at me in agreement and said that she had to stop herself from buying them every week, as the cost of the plants was depleting her modest food budget.

Her hair was fine and silky and shiny, a beautiful white with no signs of yellowing. She wore it in a loose twist at the back of her head, and several tendrils had escaped her hair pins. Her clothes were dated but of high quality and immaculate. She wore polyester pants in a soft, honey colored brown and a cardigan sweater to match. A crisp white blouse peeked from beneath the sweater, and I guessed that it had been lovingly washed and ironed during many years of use. She wore small pearl earrings and her face was carefully

Linda Hewitt
Lincolnville, ME

made up in soft, pastel tones. Her lipstick was a pale tangerine color, not usually to my liking, but perfect for her.

As we exchanged pleasantries, I made note of her stooped shoulders and dowager's hump. She had some difficulty in keeping her head erect, and she had to look up at me at a distinct angle. She was clearly a victim of osteoporosis and probably suffered as well from the insults of arthritis. She must have been much taller in her prime, but she still somehow retained her stature and elegance despite her orthopedic challenges. We parted at the store's automatic front door, each of us having decided not to purchase any plants until we saw how full our carts were after shopping.

I had moved to midcoast Maine just two weeks earlier, and this was only my second time in this small, family owned grocery store. I had my shopping list of essential items, but I decided to go methodically down every aisle, inspecting each specialty area to discover all that the store had to offer. After shopping in superstores in my former state of Massachusetts, I knew that here it would be a challenge to find all of my customary purchases and favorite brands. As a result, I was in the store for almost two hours, and this contributed to several repeat encounters with fellow shoppers.

On that particular day, as always, I spent most of my grocery shopping time in the produce section. I actually consider fruits and vegetables to be works of art (indeed, is there anything more beautiful than a perfect red pepper?), and I can't stop myself from pinching, prodding, sniffing, and examining everything carefully before I make a choice. I was peeking into the husks of locally grown corn, looking for ears with small, yellow and white, tender kernels, when the scent of Opium again alerted me to her close proximity. She too had a shopping list which she was carefully consulting, checking off each item as she placed it in her cart. I felt the need to speak to her again, so I approached her and said, "Excuse me, are you wearing Opium?" She flashed me an instant smile, then frowned slightly. "Oh, is it too strong?" she asked. "Not at all," was my reply, and I explained to her that it is a scent that I always notice because it is distinctive and reminds me of a close friend.

Our conversation turned to the subject of perfumes, in general. She seemed so pleased to have a chance to talk to someone, and I suspected that she lived alone. She told me that her daughter used to travel quite a bit, bringing home duty-free gifts of fragrances to her mother. A past favorite of hers was Shalimar, which I actually wore in my late teens and early twenties, so this established further common ground between us. I mentioned Tabu, which my grandmother wore, but she was not familiar with that particular perfume. I told her that my current favorite fragrances were Jill Sander No. 4 and Ellen Tracy, but she did not know either of them. She said that she was disappointed to learn that most fragrances are now created in the laboratory (thanks to the miracle of modern organic chemistry, with the ability to manipulate esters to create any scent imaginable) instead of using flowers, oils, and spices. She was very smart and witty, and I found myself admiring her and thoroughly enjoying her company.

We chatted easily for at least ten minutes. I began to feel that awkward need to move on, but I was unsure as to how to do it. As we finally parted, she actually thanked me for stopping to talk to her, as if she seldom had the opportunity to interact with others. I thought to myself: *Here is a gracious, refined, intelligent woman who probably spends most of her days alone. She is clearly striving to remain independent, and she is so fortunate to have retained her cognition despite her physical challenges. She appears to be in her mid-eighties, which would be the age of my recently deceased mother, but she has the spirit of a much younger woman. I wonder how she spends her time, what her challenges are, where her family is, what makes her happy.* As I finished my tour through the grocery store, I either saw her or caught her scent sever-

Linda Hewitt
Lincolnville, ME

al times. I regret that I did not ask her name, as I would have enjoyed being her friend. Never again will I smell Opium without thinking of her.

A few years after this encounter, I thought I saw her again in the veterinary hospital in which I worked as a part-time receptionist. She wore a tan raincoat, with a crisp white blouse showing beneath the collar. Her face was carefully made up, and she wore her fine, white hair in slender braids which she had wound atop her head. Accompanied by a younger woman, most likely her daughter, she was waiting for her geriatric dog to be treated. She seemed somewhat hesitant, but she stood at the counter and with a trembling hand wrote a check for Bandit's procedures. I learned that her name was Ruth. In retrospect, I realized that this could not have been the same woman whom I had met at the grocery store. The resemblance was amazing, but this woman stood straight and tall and showed none of the crippling effects of osteoporosis or arthritis. How did I finally convince myself that this was not the memorable woman from the grocery store? Well, it was simple...she was not wearing Opium.

Sally Belenardo
Branford, CT

Leaf Snatcher

Entering the woods again, I'm thankful
for nights of bitter wind
that brought the reign of color
to an end.

My walks had turned to labor,
as I gathered up the treasure on the paths.
Each leaf, unique, superlative,
detained me. I possessed

a vivid maple, divided into gold
and orange halves; the scarlet, veined
with green; the crimson, edged with plum;
brown oak, with sheen of leather; some

most typical of their kind, and those
the least. I seized bright yellow tulip,
ochre hickory, copper beech at rest on moss.
I claimed the perfect mittens

a sassafras had lost, a willow's molted feathers,
liquidambar's[*] ruddy stars.
Eyes upon the step ahead, my greed
outreached my grasp.

Now winter, growing season for shadows,
paints art I cannot steal. Every tree, a sundial,
marks time across the woods
I couldn't see, for leaves.

[*]liquidambar: tree of the witch hazel family

Debbie Budnick
Cadillac, MI

Father, Where Are You?

whimsical crying
suffocating child

where is the father
why isn't he giving any love

every second shouts out hope
every second harm is done
when just one parent flees responsibility
when just one parent is unloving

where are you father
why don't you love me

Richard Alan Bunch
Davis, CA

The One Hundred Club

Erehwon Manor, once a family residence, rises out of gray morning mists like an ocean liner looms out of a thick fog at sea. Architecturally, it is a masterpiece of Elizabethan and Jacobean design with the excessive ornamentation of the Victorian era in which it was built. It is also the scene of a biannual hunt of the One Hundred Club which provides hunting opportunities for those who have to be at least one hundred years old.

On a Sunday in December and June, they meet in town and drive out to Erehwon with their rifles and rounds of ammunition to shoot pheasant. Trees, shrubs, uncut weeds and grasses and hedges of various heights surround the manor. A swamp that was at one time a lake broods on the west side of the property with a statue of a missionary praying in front of it. There is also rumored to be a fountain of youth somewhere on the manor property. When one drinks of its waters, one ceases to get old, becomes healed, and can see at the bottom of the fountain the sacredness of water as portrayed in so many religions and folk tales all the way back to the Rig Veda of ancient India. But none of the hunters has so far found it. Or if one has found it, not one word has been said about it or its restorative properties.

I parked my car in the enclosed bull ring at the front of the manor. As I walked up the steps leading to the cricket field, I began to see some hunters at various parts of the manor grounds. One hunter in gray boots and Sherlock Holmes hat, clomped through some tall weeds at moments stalking as though he heard something about to flush out of the weeds, at others standing up as though listening to the cooing of pigeons in the trees.

At one point, I stood behind a tall shrub at the top of the lawn that sloped down to the cricket field below only to be startled by an older man with slumped shoulders and grayish hair and slight sideburn curls, who bowed low and said to my surprise: "Dr. Livingstone, I presume." I assured him I was not the famed missionary and explorer. He bowed low as though to beg my pardon and soon disappeared into a nearby thicket. It was not long before I encountered an auburn-haired man with hunting cap and ruddy face who strutted out from behind a tall pillar.

"Glad I checked first. Before I fired. I thought you were a pheasant."

"Do I look like a bird?" I said with unfeigned disgust.

"Come to think of it...you don't. Many pardons, ma'am," he said as he disappeared into a grove of trees and thick underbrush.

To say that I was becoming disgusted, not to mention apprehensive, would be a vast understatement. So far, I had been mistaken for a missionary and now a pheasant. It did not seem this brief afternoon would be all that pleasant, even if I *were* a pheasant.

I had not proceeded more than twenty-five paces when an old gentleman dressed in blue trousers, gray knit sweater, and checkered cap stepped in front of me. He wore a black patch over one eye. He stooped over and his hands trembled and slightly shook while holding his rifle that I figured must have weighed five or six pounds.

"S...s...Sonny. P....pardon me, but can you t...tell me where some pheasant are?" He tried to smile, but having only a few teeth, kept his lips closed most of the time.

"They're probably in those woods or out there in the fields," I said, indicating the long, newly-plowed, clod-knotted fields that stretched past the manor gate near a stream that ran under part of the road leading to the manor.

"I s...see. Thankee Sonny," he said as he suddenly lifted the rifle to his shoulder and swung the barrel across the horizon and fired. A large pheasant had got away with its life but the praying hands had not. They were chipped, causing

Richard Alan Bunch
Davis, CA

some pieces to fall off, and the missionary's nose had been nicked. I decided to tip toe away while he was looking the other way.

Although I made my way through low-hanging brambles to the statue of the watchful lion that slept at the back of the manor, a bullet zinged by my head. Then another. What to do? The shots stopped.

"You k...k...know somethin, s...s...sonny, I thought you was a lion." Then he laughed hard as though the whole world was laughing with him.

"No, I'm not a lion. You should be more careful. Open your eyes next time."

I left him and kept looking back as I moved away. I did not want to be shot at again.

Next to a ramp leading to the back of the manor stood an elderly gent with a head of wavy white hair who looked almost young compared to some of the hunters I had already encountered. It turned out this chap, whose name was Owyn Benflower, knew most of the hunters who regularly attended these expeditions. He seemed much younger, a relative youngster in this crew. He held his rifle pointed downward so it would not harm anyone.

"Who was that?" I asked.

"Oh, that was Nick. He gets a bit wild with a rifle in his hands. We have to keep an eye on him."

"I'll say. He almost hit me in the head," I said matter of factly.

"He does get carried away..." Owyn said.

"Around these parts, he goes by the nickname 'Nick the One-Eyed Gunner.' "

"Because he has a patch over one eye?"

"Well, he is blind in one eye. And should be wearing his glasses for the other."

"Oh, that should improve his marksmanship," I said somewhat sarcastically. Just then Nick the One-Eyed Gunner began to amble in our direction.

Richard Alan Bunch
Davis, CA

"Here he comes again," I said to Owyn.

"Hey, Nick, take it easy. You scared my friend Jack here. Your bullets nearly hit him. He ducked out of the way, you might say, in the nick of time."

After a low chuckle, Nick said: "S...s....sorry Sonny. So s...s...sorry."

"You need to be after the pheasants. That's what you came here for, Nick. They are probably over past that lawn near the woods," said Owyn, indicating a westerly direction past the cricket field and the elaborately carved tool shed.

"Thankee, Owyn. That you, Owyn?" he said, squinting, as though all he needed in the world was to focus more clearly.

"Yes, it's me, Nick. It's me." Nick gave us both a feeble salute then ambled off, holding his rifle across his chest, ostensibly in pursuit of wild pheasant.

"Have a good hunt, Nick," said Owyn.

"How can somebody whose a hundred years old be allowed to hunt?"

"Hey, I'm a hundred and two."

"You are not. I don't believe it. You don't look a day over ninety-five." I said.

"I really am. Nick's a hundred and eight."

"Only six years older? He seems much older than you."

"People age at different speeds. They really do."

"You're very clear. You speak well. He can hardly speak clearly."

"Still, it's true. I may be just like that in six years," he said, sad at the thought.

After a pause, he continued:

"But back to your original question. It's a kind of recreation for senior citizens."

"But it's not recreation to be shot at!"

"That's true. This must be your first time."

"No, my second," I said with a measure of disgust.

"You might say it's a kind of occupational therapy,"

Richard Alan Bunch
Davis, CA

Owyn continued.

"Hmmmph," I grumbled. "Too many things are done in the name of therapy these days," I said.

"We all need a little therapy now and again," remarked Owyn as he continued to scan the manor grounds for other hunters. At most there seemed to be no more than seven hunters in all, one more than the last hunt six months earlier. After a few moments my curiosity got the better of me and finally I asked:

"How *do* you stay so young? You don't look very old at all. Certainly when compared to these other hunters here."

"I'm a retired archaeologist. Taught for over forty years at the local college. Still go on digs for bones, artifacts like jewelry, and bones now and then. But for the most part I'm just enjoying retirement."

"But how *do* you stay so young? And look so young at a hundred and two?"

Owyn thought a moment. Then he surveyed the manor grounds again.

"Well, it's easy to look young when you're surrounded by fossils," he said with a slight smile.

I had to agree. He looked at least ten to fourteen years younger than these hunters out here, especially Nick the One-Eyed Gunner. He discerned from my face that my curiosity had not been satisfied so he continued:

"No, I just stay active. Keep up with the latest fossil finds. And tend to my garden of roses and tulips. Keep them well tended. Go to the Blue Rhino, a pub near where I live. Play a few round of darts with the youngsters. Down some cool brown ale like Macheson Stout or Newcastle-on-Tyne. So it's not just to be around fossils since I am becoming one myself. But to eat some really fine food. That's one of the reasons I come to these hunts."

"Really. That's why I came today. Not to hunt but to have some of that delicious pheasant. Why last time I was here the cook, I think his name is Skip, made a roast pheasant with bacon and garlic that was scrumptious."

"He puts it together, doesn't he? And Shepherd's Pie, especially when he puts a layer of corn between the meat and potato layers with a dash of barbecue sauce. Deeelicious!" crooned Owyn.

"Whether it's beef or lamb curry. Or a salad with potatoes and beetroot with goat's cheese, Skip's dishes make you forget you're here for the roast pheasant."

"And don't forget," added Owyn with gusto, "his famous dessert. Custard pie."

"You're making me hungry," I said.

"And for another dessert, maybe in our spare time, we can look for a fountain of youth that's supposed to be on the property here somewhere but I haven't found it."

"I haven't either. That would be a baptism worth dying for," I said.

"We'll have to keep hunting won't we?"

"Indeed. We sure will."

Just then a flock of pigeons that had burst out from some thick trees were greeted with gunfire. Only one was shot down. Nick's gun had done the deed. Owyn shot his rifle into the air to get Nick's attention.

"Hey, Nick! Hey, Nick!" Nick looked over in his direction.

"Did that look like a pheasant?" Reluctantly, Nick shook his head.

"Don't shoot the pigeons, Nick. We're here for pheasant. Remember that."

At that point, I decided to stay inside the manor; it appeared to be too dangerous to be outside with such hunters.

"I think I'll stay in the manor. There's some books in the library."

I understand. I should stay out here and keep an eye on these guys. You never know what might happen."

"You can say that again," I said as I walked through the large doors leading to the library with its collections of

Richard Alan Bunch
Davis, CA

Mutswairo, Shakespeare, Transtromer, Unamuno, Woolf, Swinburne, Arrabal, Goethe, Wordsworth, Lao Tzu, Dostoevsky, and Keats, movies, TV series and concerts. In a couple hours, the hunt would be over. And the grand feast, well worth waiting for, would begin.

***

Janice Marcopulos
Rockport, ME

Hanging On

A leaf hanging on to its stem
not wanting to let go and join the others.
The last wisp of wind and its gone.
Floating lifelessly to earth,
turning brown,
crinkling up,
disintegrating into the soil,
waiting for winter to come

Dee Jones
Lubbock, TX

Diamonds

On to the diamonds
We haste to run
The large and small
To heed this call

The American pastime
Best of all
Fairness is the ideal
Never needing repeal

Fun and laughter
Peanuts and such
We have it all
In the name of baseball

Be it sandlots or pros
Baseball is the game
We value those diamonds
For our fun refinements

V. Clifford Brown
Apopka, FL

The Lunch Bully

I was fourteen years old, skinny as a rail, standing by the kitchen stove watching an egg frying in the pan. I flipped that fried egg onto a slice of bread. Across the room, Mom was getting my younger brother and sister ready for their school.

I heard her say, "Cliff, what are you doing? Don't you know we have plenty of good sandwich filling? What's with the fried egg?"

"Well, Mom, I'll just smear some jam on one slice." I put the lid on the sandwich, cut it on a diagonal and wrapped it in waxed paper and dropped it into a sack. I also dropped in one of Mom's chocolate cupcakes, and I put in a napkin and closed the sack. I stuffed the apple into my jacket pocket.

Mom asked, "Are you riding your bike or are you walking to school today?"

"Bike's got a flat tire; I'll be walking. Bye, Mom. I'll be back after school."

It was one beautiful autumn day in Southern New Jersey in the year 1931. The sun was shining full in a cloudless sky and there was just enough "bite" in the air to make walking exhilarating. I had tucked my homework inside my shirt, and since the two textbooks I had taken home were secure with a strap, I juggled them as I strode along. I had to be very careful as I did not want to drop the paper lunch sack. The high school was only one mile west of town. My mind kept racing as I thought what was happening to the freshman class—what would happen to me today? Is that fried egg sandwich an act of spite?

East of town, a few blocks from our house, was a large limestone-faced church and school complex. Saint Andrews Roman Catholic Church itself was sitting on a rather high foundation. There was a beautiful set of marble steps leading to the entrance. This building had two steeples, one on

V. Clifford Brown
Apopka, FL

each side in the front. This gave it the appearance of a Mexican cathedral as pictured in our history books. I am told that the interior had many velvet draperies and the altar was covered in gold. The school buildings were located to the rear of the church. Saint Andrews, like our high school, followed the same eight-four program. That is, eight grades for elementary students and four years for senior high school students. The church had a fairly large congregation of worshipers as there were many Italian families living in the area.

Now after six weeks into the year, one student was transferred from Saint Andrews RC High School to our high school. Yancy Howard was now a member our freshman class. Apparently, his family could not afford the expense of tuition, other fees and the cost of the school uniform. He was kept attending for six weeks, but now he was terminated.

Yancy was about as tall as me but was heavier than me. He had a shock of yellowish-red hair and blushing face. Other than that, there was nothing special about his appearance. It was his unique behavior that was the big problem. He hated Vineland High School. His constant expression was "I hate this danged school." He was about as obnoxious as anybody could be!

As I opened my locker door and hung up my jacket, I placed the lunch sack on the shelf beside the books. Then a hand reached over my shoulder and a loud voice said, "I'll take that." There was no asking, no word of thanks; just a selfish grab. And so it was for a whole week. I usually ate my apple in the boys' restroom before joining the group in the gym. Yancy's taking my lunch every day is the reason for today's special cold fried egg sandwich. I wondered if things would ever change.

The freshman class had over a hundred students, but the classrooms had about thirty desks so the students were divided into four groups. For example, for basic English One, the four groups were: 1 A, 1 B, 1 C and 1 D. As luck would have it, I was assigned to 1 B. I knew only a few students there. A girl from my church who had attended a different elementary school than I did was also assigned to 1 B. We saw each other in church each weekend, but we had never been in the same school and class before. I was glad to see Carol in my class. Problem boy, Yancy Howard, was also assigned to the same class.

This kid was an expert in making paper signs and attaching them to the back of a student. He used all kinds of materials to annoy and pester people. He had a nasty habit of putting chewing gum in girls' hair. One girl who had rather long hair sat in front of him. He proceeded to take strands of her hair and weave them together, then of all things, cover the handywork with glue. He would stick out his leg and foot to trip students. Sometimes he'd bump into people very hard. He kept repeating his phrase of hating this school. One noontime, he bumped into my cousin, Roy. But Roy would have none of him. He grabbed him by the shoulder and spun him around, balled his hands into fists and gave him the old "one, two"—one left hook to the chest and a right hand punch to the stomach. Yancy gulped for air as he staggered away from Roy. He never bothered Roy again. They both avoided each other for the rest of the school year.

Parents were furious at our easy-going principal. I am sure that if my dad knew that I had not eaten lunch for a week, he would have been in that principal's face. Finally, Yancy was called before the school's judgment seat. The faculty really worked him over. Some of them wanted him expelled. But with his promises to "be good," he was allowed to continue in school. He was given a second chance.

The limited size of the cafeteria required several different "sittings." The lunch period was fairly short. Still, students had free time. The gym was a point of interest. When I arrived at the gym, some girls were jumping rope. A few fellows were climbing the rope net on the west wall. A quick game of layup basketball was in progress, and many students were on the bleachers reading or just visiting.

V. Clifford Brown
Apopka, FL

I spotted Carol sitting alone on the very highest bleacher and I climbed the steps to sit beside her. We heard the voice before we saw the boy. A loud shout, “Look at the lovebirds in the skybox.” As Yancy raced up the steps two and a time, Carol stiffened. I took her hand and leaned close to quietly say, “Take it easy, darling!” Yancy said to us, “I need help, you guys. The English teacher is requiring everybody to write an essay. I have no idea how to do that.” Carol asked him about his family. Yancy frowned and looked away. “I have a wonderful mom and a great little sister. I don’t have a father. He left us about five years ago, just drove away and never came back.”

Carol said to him, “Tell me about your sister.” Yancy looked away from us, stood up and said, “I have a little sister. Helen is five years younger than me. She has yellow hair and blue eyes and a cute little turned-up nose. I remember the first day she went to school. Mom fixed her a special lunch. Then she placed a nickel in the corner of a handkerchief and tied a knot. She told Helen to give it to her teacher to get a box of milk and straw for her lunch. She had her notebook and pencils and off to school she went. That afternoon, when she came back home, Mom asked her how she liked school. She told Mom, ‘It’s okay I guess, but I don’t know how to read yet.’ ” Carol said, “That’s your essay. Write it exactly as you just told it.”

After classes were dismissed for the day, I walked down the hall to the entrance. Carol was waiting for her mother to pick her up. When she saw me, she held out her hand. I drifted over close to her and took her hand. She said, “Did you mean what you said this noon in the gym?”

“Yes, of course I did.”

“You called me ‘darling’—no boy has ever called me that before.”

I told her, “Look, Carol, we have known each other for at least eight years, but now we are growing up. I just don’t want you falling for some handsome football player, or worse, some non-Christian scoundrel. I'm quite fond of you. I consider that you're my girl." Carol saw that her mother was waiting so she had to run. Looking over her shoulder at me, she said, "I'll think about that."

Friday, Carol and I were again on the top bleacher when Yancy came bounding up the stairs. His grin told the story. He held up a paper and said. "Thank you, thank you. Just look at this grade." He had received an "A" for the paper with the word "excellent" beside it. Carol told him, "Now when you have to write an essay, write about experiences that you have had. Make it short and end it quick." Yancy told her, "Yeah, now I know. I can tell about my dad taking me fishing, or to the beach at Atlantic City or lots of stuff." He discovered that he had a world of material to write about.

This was just the beginning of a complete change in Yancy's life. His mom had bought him a tin lunch box at Woolworth's. This box was painted with Mickey Mouse figures, and Yancy was really proud to show it off. He never bothered me for lunch again. However, he kept leaning on Carol and me for encouragement and support, and we discovered that he told other students we were his best friends.

Several weeks later, during our lunch break, Carol and I took our places on the top bleacher—the "skybox." Our curiosity was aroused as we saw the scene below us. About a dozen students were sitting on the first row, each holding his World History textbook. Yancy was standing in front of them holding his textbook in his left hand; his right hand was in continuous motion. He was walking—running in place, jumping, stooping down—he was acting out a history story. We were fascinated! We observed that Yancy's behavior metamorphosis was slowly but surely developing into maturity.

He practiced acting out scenes in the gym and he would also take advantage of time before class when a teacher was not present to stand before the class and try out his act. He was not bashful at all. Carol and I discussed how his early

V. Clifford Brown
Apopka, FL

negative aggressive behavior was now turning into a positive behavior of study and acting.

One winter day, Miss Martz, English One, passed out a dozen paperback booklets. There were not nearly enough for each student, so she measured us off in groups of three. The booklet contained the story of the sinking of a steamer, by the 19th-century author, Stephen Crane. The title of the Essay was *The Open Boat.* It is about the adventure of four survivors in a small lifeboat. The captain, the cook, the oiler and the writer, all share their fears, and hopes while drifting on the ocean.

Miss Martz was called out of the room and left us to read the essay. When she did not return after about ten minutes, the kids became restless and began to visit and become noisy. That was a cue for Yancy to take the stage. He assumed the person of each character in the story, talking to himself back and forth, often adding his own words. He had everyone's attention. About 15 minutes later, the rear classroom door silently opened and Miss Martz slipped into a nearby chair. Some of us turned to see how astonished she looked. Yancy did not stop. Miss Martz slipped out of the room but returned with the assistant principal. Mrs. Smith's jaw dropped. She whispered to Miss Martz, "To think that I wanted to expel that kid. How did this happen?"

Yancy was in demand at both Thanksgiving and Christmas holidays when the student body put on special programs. Even when he was not acting, his behavior became sensitive and courteous.

At the close of the school year at the general assembly of the student body, it was time to give out awards. Students of major sports, leaders of clubs and extra curricular activities were all honored. At the very end, the principal called out for Yancy Howard to come forward. As Yancy bounded up the steps to the stage, the entire student body and faculty all stood up. The principal presented a special framed certificate to Yancy for his outstanding achievement. Yancy stammered

V. Clifford Brown
Apopka, FL

into the microphone, "I am without words. I am surprised, of course, and I thank you for this honor." And with a bow, Yancy left the stage, waving the framed certificate over his head.

I will always remember when "the lunch bully," the rowdy, rambunctious, obnoxious, Hellion of October 1931, had become a distinguished hero of Vineland High School in June 1932.

***

Liz Moser
Baltimore, MD & Phippsburg, ME

Early Red

Dew-glinted in September sun
hung on the horizon,
a maple branch commands our thought.

Its leaves shine red although the tree
still wears the heavy green of summer.

We stretch our arms against the sky,
comb hair and view ourselves
in the mirror of our seasons, hoping
to stave off such tangible
evidence of fall.

Russell Buker
Calais, ME

Splasticity

Oh I'll bet that the rending
was nerve ending. Still, you
survived the tipsy drop-splash

from a full iceberg and now you're
keeling the berg's way through
the sands of the Atlantic while

I read in the paper that scientists
have observed a: wooly mammoth,
an extinct whale, or maybe a common

seal residing in the tip of a translucent
berg that is being monitored. Hope—
fully you can see us as you continue

your spastic steering in the crowd
that gathered to watch your ripped
Van re-enter this new world only

to secure the same helpless fate—
there is no going back—
as fired before

Charles Boldreghini
Collierville, TN

Little Lost Puppy

"I expect to pass through this world but once,"
The poet wrote.
"Any good therefore that I can do,
Or any kindness that I can show
To any fellow creature,
Let me do it now;
Let me not defer or neglect it,
For I shall not pass this way again."

Many homeless, sick or needy fellow creatures have passed
my way,
But none, save one, went unaided I'm happy to say.
Some of those that I helped I have since forgot,
But forget that one I cannot.

He was a winsome little whelp;
That one that I did not take the time to help,
It was on a country road that we met,
For that brief moment that I cannot forget.

I saw him the instant my car topped the rise,
And it was a sight that pleased my eyes.
He was stout of body and short of limb,
With large floppy ears that were too big for him.

His face I could not see,
For he was headed in the same direction as me,
Trotting along as though he knew,
Where the path beside the road was leading him to.
But there was no dwelling within a mile along that way.
"Probably tossed from a passing car," to myself I did say.

Charles Boldreghini
Collierville, TN

Well, whether discarded or lost, it mattered not.
What mattered was that he should be got,
Away from this public thoroughfare,
And put into someone's loving care.

I slowed the car as to him I drew nigh.
It was then that I heard my wife sigh.
"We've got too many pets already," said she.
And my heart grew heavy as I did silently agree.
"But," I said, "we can at least take him out of harm's way."
"If you take him home, the children'll want him to stay."

Hearkening to reason instead of my heart,
From the creature in need I did depart.
Many years have passed since that day,
But never again did I fail in that way.
And often I have wished in vain,
That I could pass that way again.

Gillian Hall
Saco, ME

Down the Wooded Path

Melanie had followed the ghost of her mother several times since returning to the house in Blue Hill, but always she lost her just as the woods' path forked in two. One route led to the ocean shore and the other off to a clearing where she and Mom had picked wild blueberries; invariably, Melanie chose the wrong path and the lost sight of the back of Mom's white cardigan, the only hint of her through the trees.

The house was up for sale as of two weeks ago. Phil had tried to get Melanie to discuss their options; the house wasn't paid off, so did it really make sense to live in the middle of nowhere now that Melanie was attending college in Orono and Phil had a forty-minute commute to work? She'd refused to talk about it, about anything at all. Mom was dead from a heart attack at fifty-three and now all that Melanie had left for family was this man who, after three years, she still felt she barely knew, and a stepsister with a staring problem. Melanie never thought Phil would make a move without her, but one morning over breakfast he'd confessed to contacting a realtor.

"This house is just too small for us, kiddo. There's only one bathroom, for Pete's sake"—Phil's chuckle was weak, diluted—"and it's so far away from everything. I understand your attachment to this place, I really do, but sometimes you've got to make tough calls about what you want to do and what you can afford. . . ."

Melanie felt sure that this was all about Phil wanting to return to Connecticut, the home he'd abandoned to marry Mom and move here with them on the Maine coast. He'd uprooted his life three years ago, leaving his relatives and colleagues behind, and now he was tearing the roots out from beneath Melanie, too. In her more bitter moments, she

Gillian Hall
Saco, ME

couldn't help but wonder if he found some small justice in that. What was Connecticut like? Melanie could only summon images she'd seen in movies, sprawling country houses with soap flakes drifting gently down outside the windows.

Mom's house was a sagging Cape Cod painted periwinkle gray with white trim. The upstairs windows were ancient, bluish, and thick, creating a sensation of peering out at the yard through a glass-bottomed boat. Melanie had never lived anywhere else, and she knew every inch of the house and surrounding woods. Over the years she'd worn paths, hung rope swings, created secret names for every landmark and shared stories with the stillness. This place belonged to her in ways that Phil could only guess at. When he'd moved in, Melanie supposed that the house had conceded to make room, the ceilings rippling above his head as he passed by, doorways buckling, aware that he was not one of the Michaud women and therefore not part of the blueprint.

In week three of the awkward, silent mourning period in which they floundered, Melanie lay in her old bedroom, listening to the fan oscillating in her window and trying to nap. A scrabbling sound came from the other side of her bedroom wall, too loud to be one of the many mice in the walls. She pushed the door open to Mom and Phil's room. "What are you doing?" She crossed to the bureau and grabbed Erika's wrist. "Why are you touching her stuff?"

Erika looked at her sullenly and wouldn't speak. She was eleven-years-old, Phil's daughter from a previous marriage. She spent many weekends and—like now—her summer vacation with Mom and Phil. Melanie couldn't imagine why Phil hadn't sent her home before the funeral; Erika had followed them mutely through the motions, hiding her face in her hair during the service and picking at her already tortured cuticles. There was eight years between the girls, and Melanie had never known quite what to make of this shy, introverted child who shared none of her interests: she couldn't swim, grew bored with hiking, and generally seemed suspicious and fearful of the outdoors. Mom had found ways around it, taking Erika shopping in Ellsworth or to a matinee. She'd encouraged Melanie to do the same, but Melanie had been sixteen at the time of the family merge and she'd had no intention of hanging around with a little kid. Now she gave the girl's arm a rough shake, wanting it to hurt, wanting to wake up those dull blue eyes. "And you better put those *Seventeen* magazines back in my room, too. I saw them on your bureau."

Erika pulled free and ran down the stairs, her escape loud and ungainly, feet thundering the steps. In the drawer were some of Mom's special things, meaningless to anybody but those who knew her best: some handkerchiefs, old birthday cards. Melanie realized that something was missing, the tarnished ring with the blue glass jewel. The little rat had taken it. Melanie turned to pursue Erika when she saw her out the window, running across the yard and disappearing into the woods. There'd be no finding her now.

The first time Melanie saw her mother's ghost, the idea of her death hadn't solidified yet among the family. They'd all moved mechanically, shell-shocked, through the casket selection, wake, and funeral. Mom had had high blood pressure for years, but no one took the threat seriously; when Phil called Melanie at the dorm to tell her that Mom was in the hospital and might not make it through surgery, Melanie had just kept repeating, shrilly, "What? What?" So when Melanie glanced out her bedroom window that afternoon and saw Mom walking across the yard, dressed in jeans and a white cardigan, her first thought was simply to go to her. Melanie pursued her into the woods, calling, and soon found herself at the shore, alone and confronted with the sight of the dilapidated dinghy half-submerged in water. She and Mom had made many a trip around the harbor this way, paddling to the little islands and rocks where the seagulls would rise, squawking at being disturbed from a spot they thought they owned. Melanie dragged the boat on shore, calling out once, "What do you want? Am I supposed to know?" to the empty shoreline.

The next time Mom appeared, Melanie had tried to follow her to the blueberry clearing and was no more successful; she'd ended up sitting on the large, flat boulder where they'd once had picnic lunches together, using the plastic tea cups from Melanie's doll set to drink from. Those times had been long before Phil and Erika, back when it was just the two of them living in the house, safe within walls that peeled paint and floors that slanted from a sinking foundation. She regretted her teenage years, when she'd strained to break free of Mom's protective grip and forge her own path, never realizing what she might lose.

Writing was Mom's passion, something she did in her free time, and when she mentioned exchanging emails with that nice man she'd met at the writer's conference in Portland, it hadn't seemed like anything serious. She'd certainly dated over the years. Mom flew out to visit Phil one weekend, and then he'd come to stay with them, a nice-enough guy with a rusty sense of humor who seemed to really adore Mom. Five months later, they announced their engagement. Despite her so-so assessment of Phil, Melanie had exploded in true teenage girl fashion; at some point during the tirade, Mom had held up her hand and said, "Melanie, this is not just about you." And Melanie had found herself speechless.

After that, graduating and getting into college had been Melanie's one priority. She knew she'd been difficult, spending as much time with friends as possible, skipping out on invitations to do things with Mom, Phil, and Erika. She'd hated seeing that hurt, disappointed look on Mom's face, the one that said, "Honey, can't you try just a little bit?" But it wasn't her style to push, so Mom had let it go, probably hoping that Melanie would come around in her own time. Now it was too late.

***

Gillian Hall
Saco, ME

Phil was waiting for her in the kitchen, preparing grilled cheese sandwiches with deliberate care. He looked rumpled and exhausted. "Thought you might be hungry." He took a deep breath as she sat. "I hope you know. . .what I was trying to say earlier is that I want you to make your home with us, in Connecticut, during vacations or whenever you want."

"This is my home."

"It's just a house. We'll find a great place back in Hartford, close to my parents, Erika's mom—something with three bedrooms, so when you—"

"I'll figure something else out."

When Phil spoke again, his voice was soft but level. "We all loved her."

"I know that!" The savageness in her own tone frightened her, and Melanie quickly left the room. She scrubbed her face at the bathroom sink and started running a comb through her hair, tugging out snarls.

Some of the old make-up that she'd left behind was missing, she noticed; cheap nail polish, some lipsticks—she could just guess who'd appropriated them. As if summoned, a faint noise made her turn and she found Erika watching her through her partially open bedroom door. Their eyes met and Erika slammed her door shut. Melanie jiggled the doorknob, found it locked, and she pictured the younger girl standing on the other side, listening. What had she done with the ring she'd taken? Hidden it? It was just a cheap thing, costume jewelry, but Mom had loved it. Melanie waited for a few moments more and then went to her own bedroom.

Time was balanced on the nearly imperceptible line between night and early morning when Melanie awoke, sweaty and tangled in her sheets.

"Rise and shine, sleepyhead," Mom said from the partially open doorway. "Come on, Mel, it's a perfectly beautiful day out there. You're wasting it."

Gillian Hall
Saco, ME

Melanie groaned and tugged her sheet over her head, something she had done a thousand times before, when she realized how very wrong this was. "Mom?" She staggered out of her room and down the stairs. Outside the window, only the faintest bluish-gray light spilled across the front lawn.

"Quit lollygagging." Mom was in the kitchen, standing before the closet as she pulled on the white cardigan she wore on walks. As Melanie stared, the scene changed—Mom was putting on a rain coat, then a down parka, then a denim jacket, flipping her hair out of the collar, turning to smile back at her daughter as she had before leaving for a thousand different walks. "Come on, Mel, no more stalling. *You're wasting time."*

"Why? Where are we going?" Once she spoke, Melanie saw that her mother was gone. The closet stood open, the bare bulb burning in its fixture. Mom's voice came again, now a toneless echo: "You're wasting time."

Melanie ran to the front door, galvanized by a building panic. She crossed the side lawn, stumbling over dips and hills that were invisible in the dim morning light. Mom disappeared around the curve of the woods' path and Melanie pushed herself as hard as she dared go, determined not to lose Mom in the trees this time. Rather than vanishing, though, the white of Mom's sweater remained, leading her on, guiding her down the fork towards the ocean.

Melanie came to a stop, half-sobbing with frustration and exhaustion when she saw that she was alone on the dock. She bent and rested her hands on her knees as she tried to regain control. When she raised her head, she realized that she wasn't alone after all; someone appeared around the side of the dock, paddling the old dinghy slowly, awkwardly. They were just a black outline in the pale light, but after a moment Melanie saw that it was Erika. The oars were akimbo as she strained to row, and Melanie could see the boat had already begun to take on water.

"Hey!" Melanie ran down the dock, waving her arms. "Get

back here!"

Without answering, the girl began paddling harder, trying to put more distance between them. She ignored Melanie's cries, making sounds of exertion as she strained to keep a boat afloat that hadn't been seaworthy for two seasons or more. There didn't seem to be any choice: Melanie dove into the water, the shock of the cold water sending her back to the surface gasping and frantic to swim.

When Erika heard Melanie swimming up behind her, she flinched back. "Leave me alone," she said, her voice high and quavering, and it was hard to tell if she was more scared of falling overboard or having to defend herself against Melanie with an oar.

"The boat isn't safe, dammit!" Melanie grabbed the side of the dinghy, trying to catch her breath. "I'll help pull you in."

By the time they had reached the shore, the dinghy was half-full of water. They watched it settle to the bottom just a few feet from where they stood. "What were trying to do, drown yourself? You can't swim—what if I hadn't been here and you'd taken that boat out deeper? Didn't you see how rotted the boards were?" Erika kept her face turned away, and Melanie took a deep breath and tried again. "What's in the can?"

The girl had had a lidded Folger's Crystals' can in the boat with her, and now she nestled it to her side, as if hoping to render it invisible. She allowed Melanie to take it. "So you were going to, what, throw it overboard?" The sandwich bag inside contained the tarnished ring, some pictures of Mom and Erika together, and a few other small notions.

"*No.* I just. . .wanted to put it somewhere safe. I was going to row out to the little island out there, where only the gulls go."

"Well, did you ever think that I might want this, too?" Melanie held the ring up, but her anger faded as she saw how hard the girl was biting her lower lip, struggling. "You were afraid that you weren't going to get anything to remember

Mom by, weren't you."

Erika plunked down into the sand and hugged her knees, rocking. She began crying soundlessly, with her mouth crimped and her eyes squeezed shut, a painfully restricted release. "You don't know," the girl said, her voice so choked she could barely get the words out. "You weren't here. Patty was nice to me. She liked me."

"I know that—"

"No you don't! You wouldn't even come down on the weekends if you knew I was going to be here!"

Melanie was speechless, remembering the times her mother would mention Erika was visiting and how she'd blithely make up an excuse to stay on campus. She thought of Mom waking her this morning, warning her that she was wasting time; maybe she hadn't just meant the moments before Erika capsized the boat. "I'm sorry. Really, I am. I've been a jerk."

Melanie sat in the sand with the girl as the sun rose, staring at the shadow of the sunken rowboat under the surface of the water. Tentatively, Melanie reached out and put her arm around the girl's shoulders and was surprised, despite her bitter words, how quickly Erika leaned into her.

The last time Melanie sensed her mother, she was in the process of packing up her old bedroom. The summer was nearly over and it was time for her to move back to her dorm room. Phil would rent a storage locker for any of the stuff that Melanie wanted to keep nearby while the rest would be moved down to the house he'd bought in Hartford. He'd guaranteed her the biggest bedroom but she'd said, "No"; it was time to stop making him jump through hoops for her. Melanie stopped packing as she realized she was being watched.

It wasn't an unpleasant sensation; it was familiar, like gentle hands resting on her shoulders, steady, approving. Melanie went downstairs and opened the kitchen coat closet,

Gillian Hall
Saco, ME

pushing through the hangers until she found Mom's white cardigan. She put it to her face and inhaled, hoping for any hint of her mother's scent, but all it smelled like was an old wool sweater. Folding it carefully, she set it aside, making a mental note to pack it with the things she was taking back to school with her. Melanie went out the front door and started walking across the still-dewy lawn towards the woods. She thought Erika might like fresh blueberries for her cereal this morning and she knew exactly where to find some.

***

Brenda Thomas
Rockland, ME

Crows

Crows danced near his eyes
On tiny delicate feet
His smile, their music.

Robert D. Erickson
Round Pond, ME

On Pemaquid

I am such a kid
When I see Point Pemaquid
Tortured granite, tossing sea
Lighthouse pulsing, pulling me
Home

***

A Moment in Time

A moment in time is gone.
All my "have to's" are done.
Another cycle of life is past.
How many more while I last?

John L. Campbell
Brookfield, WI

Finders-Keepers

Outside a suburban bank I found
her lying face down, motionless,
as if the overnight frost had killed her.
She looked dead. I picked her up

and heat from my finger and thumb
on her slim, green belly revived her.
From side to side she craned her neck,
her long, skinny legs churning the air.

People inside the bank watched,
wondering what I found so curious,
maybe a roll of green backs, as I put
the praying mantis in my pocket.

***

Russell Buker
Calais, ME

Fireflies

Incandescent land—
wash. Flighty stars:
lit stones ajar.

fireflies arrive
incandescent, lit bones;
the world's ajar.

Liz Moser
Baltimore, MD & Phippsburg, ME

Morning Moon

Morning moon.
Cold white light
across the bed
glitters behind spruce
waving in the waking wind.

Across the sky
a sense of dawn
defines the boundaries of land,
a premonition and a warning.

Already now the moon is gone
dipped toward a veiled horizon,
fast passage from a sky where
so recently it shone

Still within the comfort of
a loving arm, warm blankets,
I am awake and pulled toward day
too mindful of the speed of light.

Mary Ann Moore
Edgecomb, ME

Midsummer Day

June comes dancing across Maine with her arms full of flowers—daisies and buttercups, lupine and wild iris...

I had been in Portland all morning and was eager to get home. The day was hot and traffic was backed up for almost a mile outside of Wiscasset. I was having trouble staying awake and knew I had better stop soon for a cup of coffee.

"Excuse me, I'm a stranger here," the young man said. "Can you direct me to the bus stop?"

"Sure can. C'mon, I'll show you."

"Thanks. My name is Allen. You must be one of the glamorous summer girls I've heard so much about."

"No," I laughed, "I'm Jenny. I go to high school in the next town over.... Here we are. If you have your ticket you can sit on one of these benches and wait for the bus."

"It's not due for two hours. Will you stay for a while and talk?"

There was something about him, a sadness behind his smile, that aroused my curiosity. "I see you're in the Army," I said. "Have you just been home?"

"I've been up to Blue Hill to see my grandmother. She may not be alive when I get back."

"And you're dreading returning to the base." (The words just slipped out.)..."It's none of my business.... I'm sorry, I didn't mean..."

"It's okay." He stopped talking to look me in the eye. "You must be a mind reader. I haven't told anyone how much I hate the service."

"I'm sorry," I said again, knowing my face was red, that I should have kept my mouth shut. What in the world had come over me, talking like that to a perfect stranger? There was nothing I could do now but stick around and help cheer him up. "I know where we can get a soda and if you like I'll show you around the village," I offered.

"Yes, I'd like that."

"Leave your duffle bag in the bus station, behind the counter. Don't worry, it will be safe there."

"The tour begins on this corner," I said, feeling rather self conscious. Here is the bank and the Five and Dime. I remember one Christmas my brother and I bought all our presents at the Five and Dime—Lily of the Valley perfume for Mom and Rose for Aunt Rachel.... Would you like to go in, Allen?"

"No, I'm a last minute Christmas shopper. I'd rather go next door to the drugstore. I see they have a soda fountain."

"I recommend their chocolate sodas. They're fantastic!"

"Two chocolate sodas, please...and two more for the road."

I giggled like a little kid, "Two more! I've never had two sodas in one day in my whole life."

"Well then, today is the day to break out—try something new. Let's hope it's a good luck year for both of us."

June comes sweetly to the river-towns across Maine: the fragrance of newly-cut lawns, the seductive perfume of roses and mock orange blossoms, the juicy, berry-sweetness of strawberries...

"...and this is High Street," I announced with a little flourish. "It's my favorite place. I come here to imagine old Wiscasset. Wiscasset was once a busy port of entry and the home of sea captains. You know it was for the sea captains and their wives that these lovely old houses were built. The library is a remarkable example. I believe the house dates back to 1799."

"Drugstore, grocery store, movie theatre, library—everything is in walking distance. Neat!" Allen said. "I remember when I was a boy I had a toy village that I set up alongside my electric train. It made a pretty picture—it could have been Wiscasset."

I watched as Allen took a photo of the library. *He's a nice guy, I'm glad I stayed to talk,* I thought, wondering if my parents would agree. The rules were strict in my family. Picking up service men was definitely out of bounds. Certainly, there was nothing slick or mean about him—tall, skinny, all arms and legs; he was a kind of Jimmy Stuart character.

"You've been a swell tour guide, Jenny, you're very good at it," Allen said giving me a friendly pat on the back.

"Thanks. I liked doing it. I like history. I have a good teacher. We've been studying the early settlements. Did you know that fishermen were visiting the Maine coast a long time before the Pilgrims settled in Plymouth?"

"I've always liked studying history myself," he said, "I planned to do more at college before the war interrupted everything."

Pleased by his compliment, I seemed to lose all my shyness. I rattled on and on like some kind of salesman. "Beautiful, isn't it? The Sheepscot is a tidal river. Can you smell the sea?"

Allen wrinkled his nose. "What I smell are roses. Every garden we've walked passed has had a rosebush or two—pink, red, yellow.... If I lived here, Jenny, I would gather you a big bouquet of flowers and leave it on your doorstep...."

"... and then run away," I finished his sentence. "I'm sorry, I promised myself I would give you a happy face to take overseas."

"Do you think I'll make a good soldier?"

"I don't know. It's hard for me to imagine you marching down the street, wearing a metal helmet and kicking down doors like we see in the movies."

Allen laughed. "You've got it right about the marching. I hate having to be in step with everyone else all the time."

"My history teacher says our country needs individuals—people like John Adams and Thomas Jefferson. I think you'll do fine."

"I hope so. I'm proud to be an American."

Allen sure is different from the boys in my class at school—not a serious one in the bunch—all they want to do

Mary Ann Moore
Edgecomb, ME

is kid around.... We walked along quietly, thinking our own thoughts, until we came to the end of the street where a big mansion sits high on the hill overlooking the river.

"Wow, a castle right here in Wiscasset!" Allen took out his camera again. "Jenny, have you taken us back in time to the days of knights and ladies?"

"No, but you're right," I said, "it is a castle—Castle Tucker, built long ago by a sea captain named Tucker. I like to pretend a handsome prince lives there. For all my wishing I've never seen him."

"Well now you have. At your service, Madame," Adam bent his knee and made a sweeping bow to me right there on High Street. And then of course I had to curtsy and we got to laughing something awful.

We sat down in the field by the castle, enchanted by the charm of the place and the fun we had been having. Down on the river a lobster boat was puttering along home. A song sparrow sang from a nearby bush: 'June. June. June.' "

"Do you know today's date," Allen finally broke the spell.

"I think it's June 21."

"Well, that explains it—today is the day of the Summer Solstice! Solstice comes from the Latin meaning the day the sun stood still—a magical time.

If I knew magic, I thought, *I'd weave a web around Allen to keep him here safe forever.*

"Sometimes a perfect afternoon like this happens," Allen said half to himself, "but not very often.... Thanks, Jenny. Thanks for everything."

"It's time to go," I said trying not to cry. "I'll bet you'll do just fine in the Army."

Allen took my hand and held it as we walked down the hill to the bus station.

There is a gas station and convenience store on Route One, just before downtown Wiscasset. I bought my cup of coffee and swung the car to the right, on the little side street

Mary Ann Moore
Edgecomb, ME

that comes to such a good view of the river. I pulled over at the top of the hill and opened the coffee container.

Memories returned of an afternoon in this place long ago. In my mind's eye I saw myself and a tall, handsome soldier standing at the bus station, smiling for each other and waving goodbye.

I have come here occasionally over the years to put my mind at rest, to write a different ending to the story. June is still "bustin' out all over," the river is as blue on a hot afternoon and there is still that sweet smell of roses from the neighborhood gardens that seems to promise a world of happily ever after. But more than sixty years have passed since World War II, and soldiers like Allen continue to go to war.

Leonard Greenberg
NY, NY

Tattoo

When did it become the fashion to stain the skin
With spider's web or tadpole aging into frog,
Or boy friend ensconced in a red, red, heart.
A seaman's fad a choice of bright eyed girls.

In search of answers, I asked a punctured friend
If the pain from the needle's insertion
Could produce a desire to experience a bearable pain
To bear witness to her courage or addiction.

A buxom blonde, whose foot had grown a tree
With branches struggling to find some shade
Beneath her tight black stretch pant leg.
Between her breasts a large red rose had grown.

"Where once I might have scrawled my name,
In custom designed font and format,
To announce to all my very special being,
I spared the schoolyard wall and used myself."

Diana Levine
Monticello, NY

The Shawl

based on a true incident

My grandmother sat in her favorite rocking chair in front of the fireplace knitting a large black shawl with the wool she had in her sewing box left over from a sweater she had once made.

The year was 1912. She and my grandfather and my mother, who was 13 at that time, were getting ready to leave White Russia and come to America. A friend who was already in America was sponsoring them.

"I still have wool left over," my grandmother told my mother when my mother came into the room from the kitchen after she had washed the supper dishes. "Make a shawl for yourself. You'll have something new for our trip. Besides your old coat is too small and you need something."

"It's black," my mother whined. "Black is for old ladies."

"It's all I have," replied my grandmother. "When you're finished I'll decorate it with bits of the colored wool I still have. It will be pretty."

So my mother knitted herself a large black shawl. After she finished, my grandmother weaved some red, yellow, bright blue and orange threads through it in a flower design. "Does it still look like it's for an old lady?" my grandmother asked my mother.

"No," my mother admitted meekly.

"Ask your father," my grandmother said. My mother modeled the shawl for my grandfather when he came home. "That shawl is beautiful!" he admired. "You'll be the prettiest girl in America."

"When will we be leaving?" my mother asked her father.

"When we get a letter from our friend in America," answered my grandfather. "In the meantime, we have to pack and say goodbye to everyone we know."

Diana Levine
Monticello, NY

The letter came a week later. They were happy to be going to America but sad to say goodbye to their friends and neighbors. "We'll see you in America," my grandmother told her next door neighbor who wanted to leave White Russia, too.

On the day they were to leave they were driven to the local train station in the neighbor's horse-drawn wagon. "Don't be sad," my grandparents said when they left the wagon. "We'll see each other again in America," she repeated, hugging the neighbor.

The train took them to the seaport where they would board a ship that would bring them to New York City. Their friend would be meeting them there.

The trip on the ship was hard. The weather was cold and windy. The sea was rough. They had to sleep on mattresses on the floor. They huddled under the two warm shawls. "Aren't you glad you made your shawl?" my grandmother asked my mother one day when it was especially cold. My mother nodded.

One morning my grandfather shook my grandmother and my mother awake. "Hurry and get dressed," he urged.

"What's the matter?" my grandmother asked, fearing that there was something wrong with the ship.

"I have something to show you on deck. Hurry and get dressed. Malka, hurry!"

My grandmother and mother put their clothes on as fast as they could. Then the three hurried up the stairs to get on deck.

"Look," my grandfather said, pointing to a statue on a nearby island. "That's the Statue of Liberty. We're in America."

The three joined the other passengers cheering as the ship slid by on its way to Ellis Island.

The ship pulled in at Ellis Island. Everyone got off. My mother held her parents' hands tightly. She didn't know what to expect.

They entered a large room where inspectors were waiting

for them. They had to have a physical exam before they would be allowed to go on shore.

"I'm afraid," my mother whispered when she saw what the doctors were doing.

"Don't be afraid," my grandfather said. "I won't let anyone hurt you."

When it was their turn, my mother was very frightened and would not let the doctor touch her. "I'll hold you," my grandfather assured my mother. "It won't hurt."

The eye exam was painful but my grandfather's strong arms held my mother until it was finished. When it was done, my grandfather kissed my mother on the forehead. "You're my girl," he said. My mother just snuggled on his shoulder and cried.

The inspectors did not understand their Russian names, so they gave my grandparents and my mother names they thought were close to their Russian names. That's how they got American names.

"When are we going to see our friend?" my mother asked impatiently.

"We have to wait for a ferry to take us," replied my grandfather. "He'll be waiting when we get off the ferry."

"It's so cold," my grandmother said to my grandfather.

"Put on your shawls," my grandfather told his family.

"Where are they?" asked my grandmother. "Malka, where did you put them?"

Malka shook her head.

"Let's go look for them." Quickly they went inside. My grandmother found hers right away but Malka's was nowhere to be found.

"What will I do?" wailed my mother.

"You can huddle under mine," replied her mother, "until we get to New York City. Then our friend will find something for you."

"I loved my shawl," my mother sniffled.

"Maybe we'll find it yet," she assured her daughter.

Diana Levine
Monticello, NY

Going outside to wait for the ferry, Malka saw something hanging on the porch railing.

"My shawl," shrieked my mother.

"Someone must have found it and left it for its owner to find it," my grandfather said.

Their friend met them when the ferry docked in New York City. After greeting each other and catching up on each other's news, they left for the friend's apartment.

When they got to the building, the friend apologized. "I have to tell you it is small and the bathroom is in the hall, so I have to share the bathroom with the other apartments. But as soon as you have a job," he added, addressing my grandfather, "you'll be able to get a place of your own."

Opening up the door, they saw one large room with four mattresses laid out. In one corner was a small kitchen nook.

My grandparents gasped, but said nothing. They hadn't expected this.

"The girl needs some privacy," the friend said, referring to my mother. "I have some clothes' line. I'll nail one end to one wall near the window and the other end between the windows. Then, if I may, I'll drape your two shawls over the lines. That way the girl can have someplace of her own."

"That's very kind of you," my grandmother replied, "but that's an imposition."

"No problem at all," the friend said. "I'll get to it as soon as I get all of your luggage in."

By suppertime my mother had her own little room.

That night while they were sitting around the table in the kitchen nook, the friend told my grandparents that where he worked in a coat factory the manager was looking for more help. "I think you can get a job there," he said to my grandfather. "And I think you," addressing my mother, "can get a job modeling the coats for the people and stores who want to buy them."

"She's only 13," my grandmother interrupted. "She has to go to school yet."

Diana Levine
Monticello, NY

"In America girls her age are working already. If she wants to go to school, she can go at night. You are going to need the money."

That night my mother lay on her mattress behind the shawls crying softly. My grandfather came in and rubbed her shoulders, soothing her by telling her everything would be all right.

"What will I do when I have to go out?" Malka wanted to know, now that the shawls made up her private room.

"You and your mother will take them down during the day and wear them, then put them up again at night."

The next morning Malka and her father went to the factory with their friend.

"We got the jobs," Malka's father told her mother when they returned that afternoon.

My grandmother found a job in a nearby store. Soon they were able to find their own apartment. It had three rooms but no bathroom of their own. They had to share it with the others as they had with their friend.

"We don't need a living room," my grandmother said after they moved in their belongings and the mattresses their friend had given them. "You can have your own room," she told my mother. "As soon as we can, we'll buy beds so we won't have to sleep on the floor."

When they could afford it, they bought two beds.

"Let's use the shawls for bedspreads," my mother said. "I got a new coat as a reward for my work and I don't need the shawl anymore."

"But what about me?" my grandmother asked. "I still need my shawl when I go outside."

"Surprise!" my grandfather smiled. I got a coat for you, too."

So the shawls became bedspreads.

"There's a school on the next block," my mother said one day. "Can I go to night school?" My grandparents agreed. My mother was 14 by then. She worked modeling coats during

Diana Levine
Monticello, NY

the day and went to school at night.

One day my mother met a young man who had enrolled in night school, too. He had recently come to America. He said his parents didn't want to leave their country so he came alone. A friend of his parents had sponsored him and gotten him a job in a factory. He lived with his friend and his friend's family. He was 16. They became friends. When my mother was 16 and the young man was 18, they became engaged and got married the following year.

My father by then had become a manager of a boarding house, so my mother and he moved there. When my mother was packing to move, my grandmother urged her to take the bedspread to her new home.

"I don't need it anymore," argued my mother. "The boarding house has bedspreads."

"Take it," urged my grandmother. "You never know when it might come in handy. Besides, it comes from Russia. Don't you want to keep something from our homeland?"

My mother reluctantly agreed to take it.

"What do you need it for?" my father asked when they were unpacking.

"My mother insisted I take it. I'll fold it up and put it in the closet."

My father just shrugged.

By the following year my father was able to buy the boarding house and build it into a hotel. He also built a home for them and my grandpartents. Moving into their new home the box with the bedspreads came with them. One of the neighbors came to greet them. Seeing the shawl she exclaimed, "That shawl is beautiful. Where did you get it?"

My mother told her the story how she had made it in Russia and brought it with her.

"It's too beautiful to put away," the neighbor said. "Why don't you use it as a throw cover on your couch?"

So the shawl became a throw cover for the couch in my parents' new home.

Diana Levine
Monticello, NY

Sadly my grandparents were killed in an accident before I was born so I never knew them, but I was told my grandparents were buried together wrapped in the shawl my grandmother had made for herself.

The following year when I was born, my mother decided the couch cover was pretty enough to cover me in my carriage. She folded it to make it smaller. She got many compliments on it.

When I outgrew the carriage, it became a bedspread again, this time on my bed.

One day when I was about three, I was jumping up and down on the bed and somehow a corner of the shawl got torn.

"My shawl!" my mother shrieked. "You naughty girl. Why did you tear my shawl?"

"I'm sorry. I didn't mean it," I said, hugging my mother's knees hoping she would forgive me. Instead she sat down on the bed and put me over her knee and spanked me. Then she made me sit in the corner of the kitchen until my father came home. I was crying and begging to get up when my father entered the kitchen.

"Your daughter," my mother began, "tore my shawl—my shawl from Russia. I spanked her good."

My father said that I had been punished enough and I could get up out of the chair. "Let's look at it," he said, taking my hand and going to my bedroom. I was afraid he was going to spank me, too.

But he didn't. He examined the shawl and called my mother to come in to the bedroom. "It was an accident, wasn't it?" he asked me. I shook my head.

"Apologize to your mother," he demanded.

"I did already."

"Apologize again."

"I'm sorry, Mama," I sniffled.

Looking at the shawl again my father said, "This tear isn't so bad. I can have one of the seamstresses that works in the hotel fix it."

Diana Levine
Monticello, NY

When the shawl came back there was some gold and silver embroidered around the edge of the shawl. My mother was thrilled with the new look.

Then I don't know what happened to it because my mother put it away and I didn't see it again until I got married.

My mother took it out of wherever she had it hidden and presented it to me as a wedding gift on my wedding day.

My parents died not long after I got married. They never knew that I came to treasure that shawl. I kept it clean and repaired and wore it for special occasions.

Through the birth of my child and grandchild that shawl was kept under special cover. I took it out ever now and then just to look at it and remember my parents and grandparents and remember the stories I had heard about Russia.

One day last year my granddaughter told me her school was having a dance with an old fashioned clothes theme. I suggested she wear the shawl over her gown.

"She came home beaming," my daughter told me the morning after the dance. She said that the shawl was the hit of the dance.

"When I have a baby someday," my granddaughter asked me after that lovely evening, "can I have that shawl for the baby? It would make a beautiful crib cover."

Little did my mother know those many years ago that the shawl she made reluctantly at first would become a family heirloom that lasts to this day.

Shirely Ann Charbonneau (dec'd)
Wake Forest, NC

Left Behind

Sometime ago her husband died
which left her broken hearted.
After all those years together
she was right back where she started.

Gone forever were the dreams
they worked for through the years.
Her sleepless nights were endless
and as frightening, were her fears.

She closed herself in memories
until her thoughts depleted.
Despite words of encouragement
time...was what she needed.

In church, one Sunday morning
I saw her smiling face.
She seems to be content now,
her routine...back in place.

And as we bowed our heads in prayer
the tears swelled in her eyes.
I guess it's never quite the same
...when your loved one dies.

GOOSE RIVER ANTHOLOGY, 2010

We seek selections of fine poetry, essays, and short stories (3,000 words or less) for the 8th annual *Goose River Anthology, 2010.* Book will be beautifully produced with full color cover.

You may submit even if you have been published before in a previous edtion of the *Goose River Anthology.* We retain one-time publishing rights. All rights revert back to the author after publication. You may submit as many pieces as you like.

EARN CASH ROYALTIES. Author will receive a 10% royalty on all sales that he or she generates.

There is no purchase required and nothing is required of the author for publication. Deadline for submissions is March 31, 2010. Publication will be Fall, 2010 (in time for Christmas gifts). Guidelines are as follows:

- Submit clean-typed copy and if possible a disk (Word or WP file or if accepted you may e mail the file.)
- Reading fee: $1.00 per page (one poem per page)
- SASE for notification and possible return
- Author's name & address at top right of each page

Submit to:
Goose River Anthology, 2010
3400 Friendship Road
Waldoboro, ME 04572-6337
Telephone: (207) 832-6665
E mail: gooseriverpress@roadrunner.com
www.gooseriverpress.com

www.ingramcontent.com/pod-product-compliance
Lightning Source LLC
Chambersburg PA
CBHW020550310726
48979CB00008B/1162/J

* 9 7 8 1 5 9 7 1 3 0 8 5 1 *